Presented To:

_____

From:

_____

Date:

_____

SEVENTY
REASONS
FOR SPEAKING
IN TONGUES

Destiny Image Books by Bill Hamon

Prophets and Personal Prophecy

Prophetic Scriptures Yet to Be Fulfilled

The Day of the Saints

The Eternal Church

Who Am I and Why Am I Here

Prophets and the Prophetic Movement II

Prophets, Pitfalls and Principles III

Apostle Prophets and the Coming Moves of God

SEVENTY
REASONS
FOR SPEAKING
IN TONGUES

YOUR OWN BUILT IN SPIRITUAL DYNAMO

DR. BILL
HAMON

DEDICATION

This book is written for the benefit of the 600 million Christians who have received the gift of the Holy Spirit. The Holy Spirit's gift is the divine ability given to a Christian to pray in "other tongues" with a gifted spirit language. It is estimated that 90 percent of those who have received the gift of the Holy Spirit are familiar with less than 10 percent of the reasons for praying in tongues with their spirit languages.

This book is also dedicated to my wife and our three children who are major leaders in Christian International and to CI's great leaders around the world who kept the ministry functioning while I took the time to write this book. And finally, it is dedicated to my grandchildren and their generation, which has had little teaching on the value and purpose of speaking in one's spirit language.

CONTENTS

THE PURPOSE OF THIS BOOK

More than 600 million Christians have received the gift of the Holy Spirit, yet most do not utilize this precious gift to its full potential. And many who do speak in tongues on a regular basis do not fully understand all the benefits this gift brings. This book is being written primarily for these believers, but hopefully many who have not received the gift that the Holy Spirit has for them will also be enlightened enough to believe and receive the gift.

I am also concerned about the new generation—that of my grandchildren and great-grandchildren. Many books were written about speaking in tongues during the Charismatic Movement in the 1960s and 1970s. However, most of those books are no longer in print. The majority of Pentecostal and Charismatic ministers currently do very little teaching and preaching on the gift of the Holy Spirit with speaking in other tongues. They rarely preach on all the benefits and purposes for praying in tongues. Seeing the current lack of teaching and books on God's purpose in giving Christians a spirit language was my main motivation for writing this book at this time.

In the 1950s and 1960s, I preached much on the Holy Spirit and prayed for thousands who received the gift of the Holy Spirit.

Since that time, I must admit that I haven't preached on the value and benefits of praying with one's spirit language as often, though I have made comments about this subject in my other messages. Most of my preaching over the course of my ministry has focused on the restoration of the Church and the present moves of God. The baptism of the Holy Spirit was the main truth that was taught in the Pentecostal Movement in the first decade of the 1900s and the Charismatic Movement in the 1960s. I have focused more on pioneering and preaching the Prophetic-Apostolic Movement, which began in the 1980s; the Saints Movement, which is now underway; and the Third and Final Church Reformation.[1]

Now it has become apparent that revelation about the gift of the believer's spirit language needs to again become a priority in the Body of Christ. Recently I have taught most of what I have written in this book to the students at Christian International's Ministry Training College. I believe there is definitely a need to put the various teaching and preaching on this subject together into one volume to reveal all God's purposes for baptizing His believers with the Holy Spirit.

The purpose of this book is to enlighten Christians to the many and varied ways God intends for believers to use their spirit languages. I will cover the scriptural reasons given for praying in our spirit language. I will pull from my years of being a Spirit-baptized believer who has had many experiences in praying and ministering in my spirit language and from fifty-eight years of praying for thousands of Christians who received the Holy Spirit's gift of their own spirit languages.

WHAT IS "BAPTISM WITH THE HOLY SPIRIT" OR "THE GIFT OF THE HOLY SPIRIT?"

A Christian is "baptized with the Holy Spirit" and receives "the gift of the Holy Spirit" when the Holy Spirit gifts his or her redeemed spirit with the ability to pray in a spirit language. The spirit language originates from and is directed by the person's baptized spirit, which means his or her spirit has been immersed in the Holy Spirit. The spirit language is given by the Holy Spirit and directed by the Holy Spirit.

Paul, the apostle, explained that praying in the spirit language is a function of the mind of the spirit and not the natural mind. When we pray in tongues our praying originates and flows from our inner spirit and not from our natural mind. It is not a learned language, but a gift from the Holy Spirit. The natural mind does not understand it. *"For if I pray in tongues, my spirit prays, but my understanding is unfruitful"* (1 Cor. 14:14).

Approximately 90 percent of all that the Bible says about speaking in tongues comes from the writings of Apostle Paul. He spoke in tongues more than anyone else he knew: *"I thank my God I speak with tongues more than you all"* (1 Cor. 14:18). That is the reason Paul wrote more about speaking in tongues and the proper use of this gift than all the rest of the biblical authors. Paul is the greatest authority on the value and purpose of our spirit language.

DIFFERENT TERMS AND PHRASES BUT THE SAME GIFT

The Bible writers used different phrases to refer to the same experience and operation. The King James Version of the Bible calls it "speaking in other tongues" and "unknown tongues." Apostle Paul also called it "praying in the spirit" or "praying with the spirit." Other terms Jesus, Peter, and Paul used to refer to this experience include:

» the Promise of the Father

» another Helper

» Comforter

» Spirit of Truth

» gift of the Holy Spirit

» baptism of the Holy Spirit

» praying in unknown tongues

» praying in tongues

» other tongues

» praying with the spirit

» praying in the spirit

The expression and term that best expresses and includes the meaning of all the other terms is our "language of the spirit" or our "spirit language." I will use "spirit language" most frequently in this book to describe the gifted ministry of praying in other tongues.

THE TERMS "PENTECOSTAL" AND "CHARISMATIC"

The Pentecostal organizations called this divine experience "the baptism of the Holy Spirit," "speaking in unknown Tongues," and "the gift of the Holy Spirit." They were called "Pentecostals" because they preached that one could receive the same gift that the early Church received on the Day of Pentecost.

The Charismatic Movement ministers called this divine experience the *charismata* with *glossalalia* which caused them to be called "Charismatics." The terms the Charismatics used came from the Greek words *charismata* (meaning "the gift") and *glossalalia* (meaning "tongues"), which is another way of saying praying in an unknown tongue.

At the present time when anyone asks a Spirit-baptized person, "What type of Christian are you?" they will often say "Charismatic."

A true Charismatic Christian is one who has received the gift of the Holy Spirit with speaking in other tongues. He or she has been born again by the Spirit of God and baptized in the Holy Spirit with his own spirit language.

THE HOLY SPIRIT AND THE HUMAN SPIRIT

When the Bible spells the word "Spirit" with a capital "S" it is speaking of the deity of the Holy Spirit. When it uses the lower case "s" it is speaking of the human spirit. The lower case is used for spirit language because it is our redeemed and Holy Spirit-baptized human spirit that is doing the praying. Our spirit language is motivated, covered, and directed by the Holy Spirit, yet it is my spirit or your spirit that is actually doing the praying. This is similar to prophets prophesying or believers operating in the gift of prophecy: the Holy Spirit inspires the person to speak the prophetic words, but the person does the actual speaking. In the initial receiving of the Holy Spirit's gift, the disciples spoke in tongues *"as the Spirit gave them utterance"* (Acts 2:4); that is, He gave them the ability to pray in a spirit language from their newly baptized spirits. Paul explains it this way, *"If I pray in tongues, my spirit prays"* (1 Cor. 14:14).

So why does Paul say that it is his spirit praying in tongues? The Bible says in First Corinthians 6:17 that he who is joined to the Lord is one spirit. Our born-again, baptized spirit becomes united with the Holy Spirit, who has the mind of Christ and His Spirit enables us to pray from the mind of Christ and not from our natural minds.

When I teach on this subject I ask the audience, "When you pray in tongues is it your spirit praying or the Holy Spirit praying?" Most of the time everyone will raise their hands in agreement that it is the Holy Spirit praying. I will then have them read what the Scripture says about speaking in tongues in First

Corinthians 14:14-15, *"My spirit prays, but my understanding is unfruitful. What is the conclusion then? I* [me, my redeemed spirit] *will pray with the spirit, and I will also pray with the understanding..."* The Holy Spirit does not replace our spirit and do the speaking, but He gifts our spirit to direct our speaking in the language of the spirit.

NATURAL VERSUS SPIRITUAL

The children of Israel are God's chosen natural people. The Church saints are God's chosen spiritual people. Israel is a natural race of natural people. The Church is a supernatural race of spiritual people. Christians have a supernatural birth by the Spirit, supernatural baptism with the Spirit, supernatural grace and gifts of the Holy Spirit. What does it mean to be spiritual? It means you are born again by the Spirit, baptized in the Spirit, filled with the Spirit, walk in the Spirit, and live in the Spirit.

God made man like Himself: three in one. God is Father, Son, and Holy Spirit, three different functions or beings of the one God. Adam, the first man, was made body, soul, and spirit. Paul prayed for the Thessalonian Christians: *"May the God of peace himself sanctify you completely; and may your whole spirit, soul, and body be preserved blameless at the coming of our Lord Jesus Christ"* (1 Thess. 5:23). The Bible speaks of people being spiritual=spirit, soulish=natural self, and carnal=physical senses. I often say, "I am a spirit with a body, not a body with a spirit." This means my spirit directs and controls my body. My body is the car and my spirit is the driver. The Bible says my spirit is hidden with Christ in God (see Col. 3:3).

The Scriptures exhort us to be filled with the Spirit, live in the Spirit, walk in the Spirit, be led of the Spirit, have the fruit of the Spirit, manifest the gifts of the Spirit, and go from glory to glory until we are transformed into His same image by the Spirit of the Lord. And we live the life of Christ and manifest His works *"'not by might nor by power, but by My Spirit,' says the Lord of hosts"* (Zech. 4:6). Our spirit language is the major key that unlocks the door to our spirit life and all of the attributes and manifestations of the Holy Spirit. The whole Christian life is lived and empowered by the Word of God and the Spirit of God. The promises of God and the attributes of the Spirit are appropriated by faith. Our spirit language brings enlightenment on the Word and produces the fruit and manifestations of the Spirit. This book will contain many illustrations that reveal all the blessings and ministries that are involved in speaking in tongues in our spirit language.

A TESTIMONY OF REST

One of the couples who serves on my Board of Governors, Heeth and Jacqueline Varnedoe, wrote the following testimony. Heeth was president of a multi-billion dollar corporation before he retired. Jacqueline is a dignified, stately, southern Christian lady. This testimony comes from her new book, *Come Walk With Me*:

> Speaking in tongues carries many benefits for our spiritual lives. The more I speak in tongues, the more I flow as one with the Holy Spirit. When I am exhausted and weary, praying in tongues brings refreshing to my spirit and soul. It is like being in a flowing river on a hot day. Along with delving into God's Word and spending quality time with Jesus on a daily basis, speaking in tongues is one of the best ways to get refreshed.[2]

Apostle Paul applied Isaiah 28:11-12 to the experience of speaking in tongues in First Corinthians 14:21. Isaiah prophesied, *"'This is the rest with which You may cause the weary to rest,'* and, *'This is the refreshing.'"* Speaking in tongues causes the river of God to flow through us, bringing refreshing and rest in the Lord (see John 7:37-39).

THE GIFT OF THE HOLY SPIRIT

Prophesied by Prophets—Promised by Jesus

Prophesied:

Whom will he teach knowledge? And whom will he make to understand the message? Those just weaned from milk? Those just drawn from the breasts? For precept must be upon precept, precept upon precept, Line upon line, line upon line, Here a little, there a little. For with stammering lips and another tongue He will speak to this people, To whom He said, "This is the rest with which You may cause the weary to rest," And, "This is the refreshing"; Yet they would not hear (Isaiah 28:9-12).

Fulfilled:

In the law it is written: "With men of other tongues and other lips I will speak to this people; And yet, for all that, they will not hear Me," says the Lord. Therefore tongues are for a sign, not to those who believe but to unbelievers; but prophesying is not for unbelievers but for those who believe (1 Corinthians 14:21-22).

Prophesied:

And it shall come to pass afterward that I will pour out My Spirit on all flesh; Your sons and your daughters shall prophesy, Your old men shall dream dreams, Your young men shall see visions. And also on My menservants and on My maidservants I will pour out My Spirit in those days (Joel 2:28-29).

Fulfilled:

But this is what was spoken by the prophet Joel: And it shall come to pass in the last days, says God, That I will pour out of My Spirit on all flesh Your sons and your daughters shall prophesy, Your young men shall see visions, Your old men shall dream dreams. And on My menservants and on My maidservants I will pour out My Spirit in those days; And they shall prophesy (Acts 2:16-18).

Prophesied:

I will put My Spirit within you and cause you to walk in My statutes, and you will keep My judgments and do them (Ezekiel 36:27).

Fulfilled:

The Spirit of truth, whom the world cannot receive, because it neither sees Him nor knows Him; but you know Him, for He dwells with you and will be in you (John 14:17).

Prophesied:

I indeed baptize you with water unto repentance, but He who is coming after me is mightier than I, whose sandals I am not worthy to carry. He will baptize you with the Holy Spirit and fire (Matthew 3:11).

Fulfilled:

Then I remembered the word of the Lord, how He said, John indeed baptized with water, but you shall be baptized with the Holy Spirit (Acts 11:16).

And those of the circumcision who believed were astonished, as many as came with Peter, because the gift of the Holy Spirit had been poured out on the Gentiles also. For they heard them speak with tongues and magnify God. Then Peter answered, "Can anyone forbid water, that these should not be baptized who have received the Holy Spirit just as we have?" (Acts 10:45-47)

Prophesied by Jesus:

On the last day, that great day of the feast, Jesus stood and cried out, saying, "If anyone thirsts, let him come to Me and drink. He who believes in Me, as the Scripture has said, out of his heart will flow rivers of living water." But this He spoke concerning the Spirit, whom those believing in Him would receive; for the Holy Spirit was not yet given, because Jesus was not yet glorified (John 7:37-39).

And I will pray the Father, and He will give you another Helper, that He may abide with you forever—the Spirit of truth, whom the world cannot receive, because it neither sees Him nor knows Him; but you know Him, for He dwells with you and will be in you. But the Helper, the Holy Spirit, whom the Father will send in My name, He will teach you all things, and bring to your remembrance all things that I said to you (John 14:16, 17, 26).

But when the Helper comes, whom I shall send to you from the Father, the Spirit of truth who proceeds from the Father, He will testify of Me (John 15:26).

Nevertheless I tell you the truth. It is to your advantage that I go away; for if I do not go away, the Helper will not come to you; but if I depart, I will send Him to you (John 16:7).

Behold, I send the Promise of My Father upon you; but tarry in the city of Jerusalem until you are endued with power from on high (Luke 24:49).

And being assembled together with them, He commanded them not to depart from Jerusalem, but to wait for the Promise of the Father, "which," He said, "you have heard from Me; For John truly baptized with water, but you shall be baptized with the Holy Spirit not many days from now. But you shall receive power when the Holy Spirit has come upon you; and you shall be witnesses to Me in Jerusalem, and in all Judea and Samaria, and to the end of the earth (Acts 1:4-5, 8).

Fulfilled:

When the Day of Pentecost had fully come, they were all with one accord in one place. And suddenly there came a sound from heaven, as of a rushing mighty wind, and it filled the whole house where they were sitting. Then there appeared to them divided tongues, as of fire, and one sat upon each of them. And they were all filled with the Holy Spirit and began to speak with other tongues, as the Spirit gave them utterance (Acts 2:1-4).

Now when the apostles who were at Jerusalem heard that Samaria had received the word of God, they sent Peter and John to them, who, when they had come down, prayed for them that they might receive the Holy Spirit. For as yet He had fallen upon none of them. They had only been baptized in the name of the Lord Jesus. Then they laid hands on them, and they received the Holy Spirit (Acts 8:14-17).

And Ananias went his way and entered the house; and laying his hands on him he said, "Brother Saul, the Lord Jesus, who appeared to you on the road as you came, has sent me that you may receive your sight and be filled with the Holy Spirit" (Acts 9:17).

And it happened, while Apollos was at Corinth, that Paul, having passed through the upper regions, came to Ephesus. And finding some disciples he said to them, "Did you receive the Holy Spirit when you believed?" So they said to him, "We have not so much as heard whether there is a Holy Spirit." And he said to them, "Into what then were you baptized?" So they said, "Into John's baptism." Then Paul said, "John indeed baptized with a baptism of repentance, saying to the people that they should believe on Him who would come after him, that is, on Christ Jesus." When they heard this, they were baptized in the name of the Lord Jesus. And when Paul had laid hands on them, the Holy Spirit came upon them, and they spoke with tongues and prophesied (Acts 19:1-6).

PROMISED TO *ALL* FOR ALL GENERATIONS

The people who heard Peter's preaching on the Day of Pentecost at the outpouring of the Holy Spirit were convicted of their sins. They cried out to Peter asking, "What must we do to get right with God and receive the wonderful gift of the Holy Spirit you have just experienced?"

Then Peter said to them, "Repent, and let every one of you be baptized in the name of Jesus Christ for the remission of sins; and you shall receive the gift of the Holy Spirit. For the promise is to you and to your children, and to all who are afar off, as many as the Lord our God will call" (Acts 2:38-39).

ENDNOTES

1. Bill Hamon, *Prophetic Scriptures Yet to Be Fulfilled* (Shippensburg, PA: Destiny Image, 2010).

2. Jacqueline Varnedoe, *Come Walk With Me* (Tulsa, OK: Word and Spirit Resources, 2010), 61-62.

CHAPTER 1

WAITING FOR THE PROMISE

MAINTAINING BUT WITH MANY QUESTIONS

Peter, James, John, and the other apostles and disciples had been waiting for seven days in an upper room in Jerusalem. Each day they had all been continually meeting together, seeking the Lord and praising God. Nevertheless, I'm sure they had many unanswered questions. What was the real purpose for their gathering together in one place and waiting? What were they waiting for? How long would they have to wait and how would they know when they had received "the Promise of the Father?" They were simply following Jesus' last commandment, *"He commanded them not to depart from Jerusalem, but to wait for the Promise of the Father"* (Acts 1:4).

The following is how I imagine the events described in Acts 2 unfolded. The disciples only knew that just seven days ago they had watched Jesus ascend to Heaven. Yet just before He ascended, He had commanded them to go back to Jerusalem and wait until the Father's Promise came. Peter remembered that Jesus did not make a suggestion, but an emphatic definite command. He emphasized that this was the most important thing they needed to do. He had charged them earlier to go into all the world and

SEVENTY REASONS FOR SPEAKING IN TONGUES

preach the gospel to every creature. Now, the last thing Jesus had said was, "Don't try to fulfill the great commission until you are endued with power from on high." He told them to wait until they were baptized with the Holy Ghost and fire. But they were wondering how long they would have to wait, and how they would know when the Promise had arrived.

The disciples had risen early that morning, just a little before dawn, got themselves ready, and gathered together again. The apostles began to reminisce about how they had come to this time and place. They discussed among themselves how Jesus had called each of them to be one of His special chosen disciples, whom Jesus called "apostles." Impulsive and inquisitive, Apostle Peter asked the others if they could remember anything that Jesus had said that would give them a clue as to what they were waiting to receive. Matthew remembered that John the Baptist had preached that he was preparing the way for the Messiah. John had baptized men and women with the baptism of repentance, but told them that when the Son of God came He would baptize them with the Holy Ghost and fire.

John spoke up and said, "I remember Jesus saying that if we would fully believe on Him, out of our innermost being would flow rivers of living water. But Jesus said that He was talking about the Holy Spirit baptism, which He had not yet given to us because He had not ascended back to the Father. I remember Jesus saying emphatically that it was necessary and in our best interest for Him to leave this world, for if He did not, then the Holy Spirit could not be given to us." John continued, "I also have in my notes several things He promised while He was with us. He promised He would send us another Comforter, a divine Helper who would bring all things to our remembrance and teach us new truth by illuminating our minds with revelation. And He would give us power to do His works. In fact, I remember Him saying that if

— 24 —

we believed in Him, we would also be able to do the miraculous works He was doing, and even greater works."

James began expressing his memories, "We all experienced the full-time fellowship we had with Jesus for the last three years. We had great expectations that He was the Messiah whom the rabbis had spoken of for years; that He would come and restore Israel to be a sovereign nation as it was in the days of King David and Solomon." James recalled, "When we asked Jesus about that just before He ascended, He told us not to be concerned about that at this time, but to go back to Jerusalem and wait 'until....' At this moment we still do not know what that 'until' involves—wait until what, when, and where?"

Thomas chimed in, "I remember how disappointed and heart-broken we all were when our Jesus, whom we had trusted and followed faithfully for three and a half years, was crucified and buried." He paused. "I know I was completely discouraged and disillusioned over the whole thing. But then He appeared to many of you in His resurrected body, only I was not present. When you told me you had seen Jesus arisen and alive, I said that I would not believe He was resurrected unless I saw Him in that same body with the nail prints in His hand and the spear cut in His side."

Thomas continued, "Do you remember how He appeared again when I was there? He said to me, 'Thomas, see My hands and side, place your fingers there and touch Me and see that this is the same flesh and bone body, except now it has been resurrected into a glorified immortal human body. I am the same One who was walking and talking with you just a short time ago.' I was so overwhelmed and convinced that I cried out, 'My Lord and my God!' I am just as convinced now that since He commanded us to wait until we received that which would empower us, He will be faithful to send it in His timing and purpose."

Peter spoke up, "What else can we do? We have replaced Judas' apostleship with Mathias, which restores our number back to twelve which is the number Jesus wanted and appointed. We have searched the Scriptures and searched our minds to remember what Jesus taught and prophesied about our future and still we cannot figure out with our natural minds where, when, and how all that He promised is supposed to take place."

Peter spoke to Matthew, who, in his former profession, had been a tax collector who kept meticulous records, to check his notes one more time. Had Jesus revealed how many days they would have to wait or how they would know when they had received the Promise of the Father, the Helper, the Spirit of Truth, the baptism of the Holy Spirit? "All these descriptive statements and yet we do not know if these are several different experiences or different names for one experience that will be received during one event," said Peter.

PREPARATION FOR SOVEREIGN VISITATION

After all the confusion, wonderment, and discussion, the group decided that since they had stayed this long, they might as well continue to act on His command and keep waiting, regardless of how many days or weeks it may take before it all happened. Apostle John, the encourager, exhorted everyone, "Let us come together in unity and begin celebrating, for this is our Jewish Day of Pentecost. Our fellow Jews have gathered from the nations to come to Jerusalem to celebrate this day. It is to be a day of rejoicing and celebrating."

John continued to explain his thoughts to the 120 gathered together: "The feast of Pentecost takes place fifty days after the Passover. Jesus was crucified and buried in the grave for three days and three nights. He then arose from the grave and appeared to us many times during the next forty days, and it was seven days ago that He gathered us all together at the Mount of Olives. About 500 people were there and heard His last words and then watched

Jesus ascend up and out of our sight into Heaven. Only 120 of us obeyed His command and have daily gathered together waiting for His prophetic promise to be fulfilled. Let us all in unison begin to praise God for His faithfulness to fulfill His promises and especially for Jesus Christ. He is our promised Messiah who was crucified and rose again in order to fulfill His promise and accomplish His purpose in us."

They all began singing, praising, and worshiping God, and they continued until something suddenly happened.

THE PROMISED GIFT—NOT THE NOISE, WIND, OR FIRE BUT OTHER TONGUES

The sun had been up for awhile, and now it was about eight o'clock in the morning. As they were waiting on God in worship and praise, suddenly there came a sound like a rushing mighty wind. It sounded like the roar of a twisting tornado! Peter opened his eyes and looked over at John and asked, "Do you hear that tremendous sound of rushing wind?" John replied, "I not only hear it, but I see the women's hair blowing about their heads."

Matthew joined in by raising his voice above the roaring sound, "This is all exciting, but I don't think this is the Promise. Jesus said nothing about noise or wind, but He did say something about fire."

Peter excitedly shouted over the roar of the wind to Matthew, "Maybe that flame of fire several feet high that just appeared on the top of your head is the promised fire!" As everyone looked around, each of the 120 had a flame of fire hovering over them. From a distance it looked like the whole upper room was on fire, for the flaming light was brighter than the sun.

John spoke, saying, "These flames of fire are wonderful to see and thrilling to experience, but still I do not think this is what Jesus promised. He said it would come to be 'in us and flow out of us like a river' and that would be the promised gift of the Holy Spirit."

THE PROPHETIC PROMISE
FINALLY FULFILLED

Before John could finish talking, suddenly the Holy Spirit came into each one of them, and they all began to speak in tongues. One moment John was speaking in Hebrew, and in the next instant he was speaking in other tongues. The Holy Spirit had just baptized them by giving each person present in the upper room his or her own spirit language.

They all continued speaking in tongues over the next hour. Their time of persistently waiting had paid off. The Promise had been sent, the Holy Spirit had come, and the gift of the Holy Spirit was now received and activated into manifestation. The river of living water was flowing out of their innermost beings. It was a river of abundant life and such joy that it could not be expressed in their native tongue but was being expressed with their spirit languages. There was such a surge of power that they spoke out in tongues loudly and for a long time. It was so fulfilling and satisfying, after having to wait so long, that it made them desirous to continuously pray, praise, and magnify God with their new spirit languages.

SUPERNATURAL MANIFESTATION
ATTRACTS PEOPLE

While the 120 believers in the upper room were excitedly praising God in their new languages of the Spirit, things were happening in the streets below. Jerusalem was full of people, as many Jews from outside the city had come to participate in the Feast of Pentecost. The great roaring sound of wind and the brilliant light of 120 flames of fire that preceded the disciples receiving the gift of the Holy Spirit had attracted a great crowd of people. The wind and fire had faded away, but the noise of the 120 praying in tongues could be heard for blocks in all directions. Several thousand Jews gathered around the building with the majority in the big open area in the front.

The newly baptized disciples had been speaking in tongues for almost an hour when the sound of the crowd from below penetrated Peter's conscious mind. He walked out onto the balcony and was surprised to see a great crowd of people had gathered. Some were yelling, "What's happening up there?" Others were saying, "They all must be drunk to be acting that way and making that much noise." Others replied, "They are not likely to be drunk as it is only nine o'clock in the morning. People do not gather to get drunk in the morning, but at night."

Then the crowd began to quiet down and listen more intently. They were amazed at what they were hearing! It was not just nonsensical noise; the listeners could understand what some of the believers were saying. The crowd consisted of Jews from many nations who spoke not only Hebrew, but also the languages of the nations in which they were born. They were amazed, for each Jew heard some of the 120 speaking in his national home language. The amazing thing was that all those speaking in the different languages were Galileans, and the majority of them only knew one learned language.

The doubters and skeptics among the crowd were still ridiculing, mocking, and accusing the disciples of being drunk or something similar. But the majority were saying, "That cannot be the case. This is creating a holy, peaceful atmosphere, and the ones we can understand are speaking words describing the wonderful works of their Jehovah God. They are praising His majestic glory and glorious power." They began to say, "This is something mighty to behold. But what does it mean?"

PREACHING EXPLAINS WHAT HAS PROPHETICALLY HAPPENED

When Peter stepped out onto the big balcony, he listened for a while to what the crowd was saying. He felt inspired to answer their inquiries and explain to them what was happening. The other apostles joined Peter on the balcony as he began to preach to that great gathering of Jews. He preached a long message, some of which is not recorded, but the following are some highlights of what was recorded. Peter proclaimed to these Jews that Jesus Christ of Nazareth was their long-awaited Messiah, but their leaders had Him crucified. Jesus was crucified, but He rose again. Peter quoted several Scriptures to prove that Jesus was the Messiah.

He then prophetically explained to them, "What you are seeing and hearing is a fulfillment of the prophecy of the Prophet Joel, what John the Baptist prophesied, and what Jesus prophetically promised." He explained it this way, "This Jesus God has raised up, of which we are all witnesses. Therefore, being exalted to the right hand of God, and having received from the Father the promise of the Holy Spirit, He poured out this which you now see and hear." Peter said in his closing comments, *"Therefore let all the house of Israel know assuredly that God has made this Jesus, whom you crucified, both Lord and Christ"* (Acts 2:36).

When they heard his anointed message, great conviction came upon them and they cried out to Peter, "What shall we do? What must we do to take away our guilt and sin and receive the wonderful gift of the Holy Spirit that you have been manifesting?"

A TRUTH AND PROMISE FOR ALL GENERATIONS

Peter's answer to the inquiring Jews has become an established truth for all generations: "Everyone of you must repent and be baptized in the name of Jesus Christ for the remission of sins, and then you can receive this gift of the Holy Spirit. For the promise is unto you and to all future generations. For as many as the Lord shall call for salvation are also called to receive the gift of the Holy Spirit."

About 3,000 people in the crowd believed and were baptized in the name of their newly discovered Messiah and Savior, Jesus Christ. In one day the Church was born as the number of believers grew from 120 to 3,000. This fulfilled the prophecy of Isaiah that a nation would be born at once in one day (see Isa. 65:8). This all happened because of God's Promise, Jesus' provision, man's preparation, and Heaven's participation.

HEAVEN'S VIEW AND PARTICIPATION

Whenever God does something special on the earth, His heavenly host of angels work with Him. Certain activities on earth cause corresponding activity in the heavenlies. Several illustrations in both the Old and New Testaments reveal this reality.

When the four leprous men in Two Kings chapter seven started marching toward the Syrian army, Heaven's angelic army began marching above them in the heavenly realm. God allowed the Syrians to hear the sound of a million soldiers marching, the sound of horses and chariots, and the thunderous shouts of warriors. The sound was so frightening that they fled for their lives leaving everything behind. The four leprous men came and gathered some of the Syrian army's wealth and then let the besieged city of Samaria know about the abundance (see 2 Kings 7:1-29).

David received direction from the Lord on how to win his battle against the Philistines. God told him he would know the time to launch the battle—it would be when the heavenly angelic armies began to advance against His enemies. This is the way King David would know they were positioned above him in the heavenlies and moving toward the battle: he would hear and see the tops of the mulberry trees swaying forward as if a strong wind was blowing. When David saw that, he and his army engaged the Philistines in battle and won a great victory. In the spirit world, God's angelic army defeated the evil army of Satan's angels that was with the Philistines, while on earth David and his warrior soldiers defeated the Philistine soldiers (see 1 Chron. 14:8-17).

When Prophetess Deborah and General Barak fought with Sisera, commander of the Canaanite army, God's heavenly army and nature worked with them to win the battle. God's heavenly army provided the air force while Deborah's human army provided the ground troops who destroyed the evil army and possessed the land (see Judg. 4:1-24).

At the most important event ever to take place on planet earth, a great multitude of angels flooded the area around Bethlehem during the birth of Jesus. They extended all the way from the manger in Bethlehem to outside the city where shepherds were tending their sheep (see Luke 2:8-20).

ANGELS ARE WARRIORS AND MINISTERS FOR THE HEIRS OF GOD'S SALVATION

The Bible says that God's angelic spirit beings are commissioned to minister to those members of God's humankind creation who are called to receive and demonstrate His great salvation (see Heb. 1:13-14; 2:2-3). Angels make divine announcements, war against evil forces, clear the atmosphere, and saturate it with God's presence for the fulfilling of God's purposes (see Luke 1:26-38; Dan. 9:21; 10:13). With this biblical insight concerning angels and their participation in God's work on earth, let us go back in time to the Day of Pentecost where all of Heaven was in attendance and involved in the birth of Jesus' beloved Church.

As all of the heavenly host had been present and participating at the birth of Jesus, now they were all gathered at Jerusalem for the birth of Jesus' beloved Church. The Holy Spirit had already arrived with His gift that would empower the new Spirit-born Church to begin immediately talking in their spirit languages. We will now view what was taking place in the heavenlies while the Church was being birthed on earth.

HEAVEN'S PARTICIPATION IN THE BIRTH OF THE CHURCH

For the past fifty days there had been much more angelic activity around Jerusalem than usual. But as the sun began to rise on the Day of Pentecost, multitudes of angels began descending from Heaven. Mighty divisions of the armies of Heaven began to position themselves to participate in the great event that would take place this day in Jerusalem. Heaven had been watching and listening to the small group gathered in the upper room. A short time after eight in the morning, the disciples ceased their discussions and joined together in unity and accord to praise and magnify God.

Suddenly, God the Father raised His hand to signal that the appointed time had arrived. Jesus, the Commander of all the heavenly armies, gave an excited commanding shout, "The time has arrived for the birthing of My beloved Church, which I purchased with My own blood!" The Archangel Michael, the general of the angelic army, positioned himself to lead the army. The Archangel Gabriel lifted his special events trumpet to his lips and began trumpeting the appointed time. Millions of angels began descending straight down from Heaven like a great waterfall heading straight for the upper room in Jerusalem.

As the angels descended toward the upper room, they suddenly exploded into all directions. With light brighter than the sun, it looked like an atomic bomb exploded. The divine light removed all the spiritual darkness as the rising sun had removed all natural darkness. The force of the great army of angels moving out in all directions cleared the atmosphere of all evil forces and saturated the area with the presence of God. A portion of the angels fulfilled their assignments by roaring into the room on the wind of the Spirit. Other angels carried flames of fire, which they placed on the heads of each of the disciples.

The Holy Spirit flooded into the upper room and baptized everyone, giving each believer his or her gift of other tongues, which enabled them to begin speaking the wonderful works of God in a new spirit language.

THE PATTERN AND PRACTICES REMAIN THE SAME

When God gave Moses the pattern for the Tabernacle, He commanded him to make sure he made it exactly according to the pattern. God gave Moses the Law and all of its ceremonies, sacrifices, and feasts, which were to be practiced during the dispensation, or age, of the Law. The dispensation of the Law ended when the age of the Church began. The Law became the Old Covenant of God with His Israelite people while God's New Covenant was with His new people called the Church. The Church Age started when Jesus came and purchased the Church with His blood, authorized it by His resurrection, and birthed and empowered it on the Day of Pentecost with His Holy Spirit (see Acts 20:28; Rom. 1:4; Acts 1:4, 8; 2:4).

The age of the mortal Church will continue until the second coming of Christ Jesus. When Jesus returns, He will resurrect and translate the mortal Church into the immortal Church. The pattern, principles, and spiritual practices that are established at the beginning of a new covenant of God remain the same during the duration of that covenant. All the teachings, practices, and spiritual experiences of the Church, as recorded in the New Testament of the Bible, are for the entirety of the mortal Church Age.

The Church started with its members speaking in tongues. Believers have continued receiving the gift of the Holy Spirit with the ability to pray in a spirit language, and the Church will finish with praying in tongues. Speaking in tongues was a practice established in the foundation of the Church. First John 5:8 says there are three things that bear witness on the earth: the blood, the water, and the Spirit. The witness of the blood of Jesus comes with the baptism of repentance. The witness of water comes with water baptism in the name of the Lord Jesus. The witness of the Spirit comes with the baptism of the Holy Spirit. The doctrine of baptisms is the third of the six major doctrines of Christ, which are foundational blocks of the Christian faith (see Heb. 6:1-2). All three witnesses and baptisms are still valid and present practices in the Church.

The gift of one's spirit prayer language comes with the baptism of the Holy Spirit. The gift of the Holy Spirit is for every Christian to receive and practice, just as every Christian is to receive water baptism. The Holy Spirit's gift of speaking in tongues is part of the practices and doctrines of the New Testament Church. Therefore, it is essential that we be thoroughly established in the biblical truth of the gift of the Holy Spirit, its purpose, and all of the valuable benefits of praying in our spirit language.

CHAPTER 2

70 Reasons for the Holy Spirit's Gift of Speaking in Tongues

Two Reasons from Chapter 1

One

The 120 disciples, including the apostles, obeyed Jesus' command to wait until they received. Jesus promised they would receive the Promise of the Father, the Helper, the Spirit of Truth, the Baptism of the Holy Spirit. They had heard all these descriptive statements, and yet the apostles did not know if they were different experiences to be received at different times or various names describing the same experience that would be received during one event. It proved to be one experience received at one time when they all began to speak in tongues. From then on the apostles prayed for people to receive the gift of their own spirit languages and established speaking in tongues as proof that a person had received the gift of the Holy Spirit (see John 14:16-17, 26; 16:7; Luke 24:49; Acts 1:4).

Two

The gift of the Holy Spirit is for every Christian to receive and practice just as every born-again Christian is to receive water baptism. The Holy Spirit's gift of speaking in tongues is part of the practices and doctrines of the New Testament Church. Therefore it is essential that we be thoroughly established in the biblical truth of the gift of the Holy Spirit, know its purpose, and understand all of the valuable benefits of praying in our spirit language (see Heb. 6:2; Acts 2:38; 1 Cor. 14:14).

FIFTEEN BIBLICAL PROOFS FOR BELIEVING AND SCRIPTURAL REASONS FOR RECEIVING THE HOLY SPIRIT GIFT

THREE

The gift of the Holy Spirit or the Holy Spirit Gift, which was prophesied by the prophets, applied to "tongues" by the Apostles. God planned to give the saints the gift of their own spirit languages when He chose us in Christ before the foundation of the world (see Eph. 1:4). Apostle Peter applied Joel's prophecy about how God would pour out His Spirit upon all flesh to the Day of Pentecost when the disciples received the gift of the Holy Spirit (see Joel 2:28; Acts 2:16). Apostle Paul applied Isaiah's prophecy of God speaking to His people with stammering lips and other tongues to the Holy Spirit's gift of speaking in tongues (see Isa. 28:9-12; 1 Cor. 14:21). Jesus told His followers that at that time He was with them but when He sent the Holy Spirit to them He would be in them. This was a fulfillment of Ezekiel's prophecy that God would give to those who would be His people a new heart and a new spirit and then He would put His Spirit within them (see Ezek. 36:27; John 14:17; Col. 1:27).

FOUR

John the Baptist, who prepared the way for the coming of Jesus the Messiah, also prophesied that Jesus would baptize His followers with the Holy Spirit and fire. This was important enough to

God to have the prophet, John the Baptist, describe Jesus as the Baptizer with the Holy Spirit as well as the Lamb of God who takes away the sin of humankind (see Matt. 3:11-12; Mark 1:6-8; Luke 3:15-16; John 1:12-13).

FIVE

Jesus promised several times that He would send the promise of the Father, which is the Holy Spirit's gift of the spirit language. Jesus had to die, be resurrected, and ascend back to the Father in order to send this gift. All who have received cleansing from sin by the life blood of Jesus should be more than willing to die to human pride and religious prejudice and receive what Christ died to give. Praying in tongues crucifies the flesh and humbles the pride of man. Jesus paid a great price in order to fulfill His promise of sending the gift. That should be reason enough for all Christians to receive this gift (see John 16:7; Rom. 5:10; 1 Pet. 5:6).

SIX

The terms listed below are synonymous with the gift Jesus promised to send back to His faithful followers. Actually we discover by the fulfillment of that promise that Jesus was saying in effect, "I am sending you the Holy Spirit for My universal Church, but the Spirit is bringing His special gift for the individual believer." All the following are different words describing the same Holy Spirit experience and gift of the spirit language:

The Holy Spirit (see Matt. 3:11; John 7:39; 14:26; Acts 1:5, 8; 2:4, 33, 38; 5:32; 9:17; 10:44-45, 47; 11:15, 16, 24; 19:26).

» The Spirit of Truth (see John 14:17; 16:13)

» The Comforter/Helper (see John 14:16, 26; 15:26; 16:7)

» The Promise of the Father (see Luke 24:49; Acts 1:4)

» Be baptized with the Holy Spirit (see Acts 1:5)

» Gift of the Holy Spirit (see Acts 2:38; 10:45)

» Holy Spirit of Promise (see Eph. 1:13)

SEVEN

The manifestation that came with the gift of the Holy Spirit was speaking in tongues. It was not the wind, fire, noise, or feeling God's presence that was the evidence of the gift being received, but the spirit language that caused the believers all to begin speaking languages of the Spirit that they did not understand. Nonetheless, they were speaking of the wonderful works of God in their unlearned languages. It was God's plan for the gift to function as a spirit language for His children. God wanted it that way and that is reason enough to receive the gift and let it function His way (see Acts 2:4,11; 1 Cor. 14:2).

EIGHT

Speaking in tongues was the sign that Christ's Church had just been born. When a human baby is born the first thing he does is to start breathing and expressing with his mouth—usually by crying. The first thing that Jesus' newborn Church did was to breathe the breath of life and begin expressing themselves with their mouths by speaking in tongues. The new spirit language is the native tongue of the citizens in the Church of the firstborn (see Acts 2:4; Heb. 12:23).

NINE

The Gentiles speaking in tongues is what convinced the Apostle Peter that Gentiles could become children of God without becoming proselyte Jews first. When the gentile household of Cornelius believed Peter's preaching, the Holy Spirit suddenly baptized them. What proved to Peter that Jesus had just saved the Gentiles and the Holy Spirit had baptized them was not that they suddenly had peace or joy or excitement, but it was that he "heard them speaking with tongues." When Peter arrived back at Jerusalem to give his defense before the other apostles for ministering to Gentiles, he gave this report:

> *And as I began to speak, the Holy Spirit fell upon them, as upon us at the beginning. Then I remembered the word of the Lord, how He said, 'John indeed baptized with water, but you shall be baptized with the Holy Spirit.' If therefore God gave them the same gift as He gave us when we believed on the Lord Jesus Christ, who was I that I could withstand God?"*

> *When they heard these things they became silent; and they glorified God, saying, "Then God has also granted to the Gentiles repentance to life."*

> *Now those who were scattered after the persecution that arose over Stephen traveled as far as Phoenicia, Cyprus, and Antioch, preaching the word to no one but the Jews only. But some of them were men from Cyprus and Cyrene, who, when they had come to Antioch, spoke to the Hellenists, preaching the Lord Jesus. And the hand of the Lord was with them, and a great number believed and turned to the Lord.*

> *Then news of these things came to the ears of the church in Jerusalem, and they sent out Barnabas to go as far as Antioch. When he came and had seen the grace of God, he was glad, and encouraged them all that with purpose of heart they should continue with the Lord (Acts 11:15-23).*

The early apostles were convinced that God had accepted the Gentiles because they heard them speak in tongues just like they had spoken in tongues on the Day of Pentecost when they received the gift of the Holy Spirit. That should be proof and reason enough for us to be convinced that speaking in tongues was the consistent manifestation that the apostles recognized as the evidence that a person had received the promised gift of the Holy Spirit (see Acts 10:34-48; 11:1-18).

TEN

Apostle Paul received the gift of the Holy Spirit when Ananias laid hands on him and prayed for His healing. Ananias said, *"The Lord Jesus has sent me that you may receive your sight and be filled with the Holy Spirit"* (Acts 9:17). Paul received the Holy Spirit's gift at the same time the scales fell from his eyes. Paul greatly appreciated receiving his spirit language. During the following years as he discovered all the purposes and spiritual benefits of praying in tongues, he became so thankful that he spoke in tongues. It motivated him to emphatically declare to the Corinthian church, *"I thank my God I speak with tongues more than you all"* (1 Cor. 14:18).

Paul wrote more about speaking in tongues than all the other authors of the books of the Bible. Paul's abundance of speaking in tongues is what helped activate the spirit of wisdom and revelation within him, which empowered him to work miracles and be inspired to write fourteen of the twenty-seven books of the New Testament.

Speaking in tongues was good enough for Paul and the other apostles and saints of the New Testament Church, so it is good enough and important enough for each of us to receive and pray much in our spirit language. Praying in tongues cannot and will not make you operate in a ministry that God has not planned for you, but it can enlighten and empower you with all the wisdom and ability you will need to fulfill your calling. Seeing how the spirit language helped produce Paul's powerfully successful life and ministry should be more than reason enough for us to want to receive the gift and pray in our spirit language longer and more often (see Acts 9:10-19).

ELEVEN

Speaking in tongues was a vital part of the gospel Paul preached. The gospel is the death, burial, and resurrection of Jesus Christ, which a believer identifies with in the three baptisms of repentance, water, and the Holy Spirit. The large local church at Corinth is typical of the numerous churches Paul pioneered. His letters to them reveal what he taught and the spiritual experiences he ministered to them. The Corinthian Christians were so active in speaking in tongues and manifesting the gifts of the Spirit that Paul had to devote two chapters to give them wisdom concerning speaking in tongues in private and speaking in tongues in the assembly of saints. His concluding statements in chapters twelve and fourteen on this subject were, *"Desire earnestly to prophesy and forbid not to speak with tongues"* (1 Cor. 14:39). (See 1 Cor. 15:1; Rom. 15:19, 29.)

TWELVE

Paul made sure those who had only believed on the Messiah also received the gift of the Holy Spirit. When he met twelve Baptist believers (followers of John the Baptist), he asked them if they had received the Holy Spirit since they believed. They said that they had not heard about a Holy Spirit baptism. They explained they had only received the John-the-Baptist baptism, but they wanted all God had for them. Paul baptized them in water in the name of the Lord Jesus. And when he laid his hands on them they received the gift of the Holy Spirit and began speaking in tongues and even prophesied.

Being baptized with the Spirit is a separate experience from being born of the Spirit or water baptism. There are three different baptisms or works of the Holy Spirit. We who have the gift of the Holy Spirit need to enlighten all the Christians who have not received and pray for them to receive the gift with speaking in tongues. It is not proselyting or imposing ourselves on others, but simply helping God's children receive all that Jesus provided for them. Part of the purpose of this book, especially these scriptural proofs, is to help you show Christians that this experience is biblical and for them today. Jesus told the disciples that when they received the gift of the Holy Spirit that they were to witness to others (see Acts 1:8; 19:1-7).

THIRTEEN

The apostles at Jerusalem believed in the need for new converts to receive the gift of the Holy Spirit after they had been saved and baptized in water. Philip the Evangelist went to Samaria and preached the gospel to the people there. Many received salvation, healing, demonic deliverance, great joy, and water baptism.

> *Now when the apostles who were at Jerusalem heard that Samaria had received the word of God, they sent Peter and John to them, who, when they had come down, prayed for them that they might receive the Holy Spirit. For as yet He had fallen upon none of them. They had only been water baptized in the name of the Lord Jesus. Then they laid hands on them and they received the Holy Spirit. And when Simon saw that through the laying on of the apostles hands the Holy Spirit was given, he offered them money* (Acts 8:14-18).

When Simon, the former sorcerer, saw that the Holy Spirit gave believers the ability to speak in other tongues, he offered the apostles money to give him that ability. He had not offered money to Philip to be able to perform the signs, wonders, and miracles that were accomplished through his ministry, for Simon had performed signs and wonders when he was a sorcerer. But this was something he had never seen or done. By the apostles simply laying their hands on the new converts to Christ they began to speak in other tongues with a spirit language. It had to be speaking in tongues as that is the only consistent manifestation that happens when a person receives the gift of the Holy Spirit. The early apostles felt it necessary to make sure every Christian convert received the gift of the Holy Spirit, as should every Christian minister in the twenty-first century Church should have the same conviction, mandate, and ministry (see Acts 8:1-25).

FOURTEEN

To receive the gift of the Holy Spirit is a commandment of Jesus Christ. When Jesus commissioned the disciples to wait in Jerusalem until they received the promise of the Father, He did not say, "Do this if you feel led to do so, or if it fits in your doctrinal or denominational beliefs, or if you have the time, or are so inclined or feel comfortable about it." No! Jesus commanded them to wait until they received the gift of the Holy Spirit. He was conveying the reality that there was nothing more important for them to do than to receive the Holy Spirit. Since Jesus put such importance on the need for receiving the Holy Spirit's gift, then that is more than enough reason for every Christian to keep seeking God until they receive their spirit prayer languages evidenced by speaking in tongues. Jesus said, "If you love me keep my commandments."

Jesus gave three major commandments: First, love the Lord your God with all your heart, soul, mind, and strength. Second, love your neighbor as you love yourself. Third, wait for the promise of the Father until you are filled with the Holy Spirit. The Holy Spirit is only given to those who obey Jesus' command to believe and receive the gift of the Holy Spirit (see Acts 1:4; 5:32; John 14:15-17; Eph. 5:18; Matt. 22:36-40; Mark 12:28-31).

FIFTEEN

Mark declares in his Gospel that Jesus told believers to go into all the world and preach the gospel to every creature. There would be certain signs to evidence those who had become believers in the full gospel they preached. Those who believed would be saved and baptized in water, and one of the signs that would follow would be, "They shall speak with new tongues." From all that happened on the Day of Pentecost and during the following years, Jesus was speaking about the gift of the Holy Spirit, which is evidenced by "speaking with new tongues." God confirmed the word the believers preached with accompanying signs. Speaking in tongues was an accompanying sign. Believers do not follow after signs, but signs do follow them, and one of those signs is speaking in tongues (see Mark 16:14-20).

SIXTEEN

The Scriptures exhort us to be filled with the Spirit and pray in the new tongues of our spirit language, which enables us to live in the Spirit, walk in the Spirit, be led of the Spirit, have the fruit of the Spirit, manifest the gifts of the Spirit, and go from glory to glory until we are transformed into His same image by the Spirit of the Lord (see Gal. 5:22-25; Rom. 8:14; 1 Cor. 12:7-11; 14:15; Eph. 5:18; Acts 19:2; 2 Cor. 3:18).

SEVENTEEN

The gift of the Holy Spirit or the Holy Spirit's gift is the divine ability given to a Christian believer to pray in a supernatural language of the Spirit. Some of the other terms used to describe the operation of this gift are praying in unknown tongues, praying in other tongues, praying with the Spirit, and praying in the Spirit. The term that best covers all these is the believer's spirit language (see 1 Cor. 14:14-18; Acts 2:4; Eph. 6:18). The seventy (70) reasons for speaking in tongues (our spirit language) will be continued at the end of each chapter.

CHAPTER 3

THE GREATEST GIFT

THE GODHEAD IS A GIVING GOD: THE GIFT EACH GAVE

The eternal Godhead of Father, Son, and Holy Spirit are one. *"For there are three that bear witness in heaven: the Father, the Word* [the Son was the Word made flesh] *and the Holy Spirit; and these three are one"* (1 John 5:7). This reveals that whenever we speak of God as the Father, Son, or Holy Spirit we are talking about the same nature, attributes, power, and love. All that God is, all three are.

God is a Giver, and He always gives His best. Each member of the Godhead gave His greatest possible gift to humankind. So when we ask, "Why did God do it?" we are really asking, "Why did each of Them give the gift He gave?" Each gift was given with the same love motivation for the benefit of the one receiving the gift, and it is the best and greatest gift that could possibly be given. Father God's gift of His Son was His best for the world; Jesus the Son's gift of the Holy Spirit to the Church was the best He could possibly give; and the Holy Spirit's gift of the spirit language was the best and greatest gift for the individual believer. This book is dedicated to discovering and revealing all the benefits of our spirit language so we can understand why it was the best gift the Holy Spirit could give to bless and empower the Christian believer.

GOD THE FATHER'S GIFT

For God so loved the world that He gave His only begotten Son that whoever believes in His Son, Jesus Christ, would receive everlasting life (John 3:16). Father God gave His Son as a gift for the redemption of the world. Why did God do it? Why does God do what He does? The answer is because God is love. The love of God is a giving love. True divine love gives its best. God the Father so loved...that He gave His only begotten Son. Jesus was nearest and dearest to the heart of God. There was not a greater gift from His whole Being and eternal universe that God could give. For God to give Jesus was to give Himself. God's past, present, and future was centered in His Son. Jesus was the fulfillment of all of God's desire and purpose.

We need to take notice that God's "so loved" included His masterpiece creation of humankind and the world of Earth and all that He created on it for man's home and headquarters. God not only loved the people in the world, but He also loved the world He had originally created for man's dwelling place. Earth was the place where the original man and woman were created. Adam's body was created from the dust of the earth; Eve was created from the body of man. They were commissioned to be fruitful and multiply the human race upon the earth. The Bible declares that the earth is the Lord's and everything in it. Romans 8:19-23 declares that when the children of God receive the redemption of their bodies, then the whole natural creation of God will be redeemed.

However, nothing is more important to Father God than His masterpiece creation of humankind, whom He created in His own image and likeness. Adam was God's created son whom God formed with His own two hands, then breathed into him the breath of life. But Jesus was Father God's only begotten Son, the only human being born into this world who was fathered personally by God Himself. God gave this only begotten Son for the reconciling of the world. "God was in Christ reconciling the world to Himself" (2 Cor. 5:19). The gift that God gave was His only begotten Son and His gift was given for the redemption of humankind and all creation.

GOD THE SON'S GIFT

Jesus willingly did the Father's will and became the Lamb of God slain for the redemption of humankind and the world. The Bible does not talk about Jesus loving the world, but about Him loving the Church. The Scripture declares that Jesus Christ loved the Church and gave Himself for the Church that He might present her to Himself a glorious Church (see Eph. 5:25-27). Jesus loved the Church more than He loved life itself for He gave His life's blood to purchase the Church. *"Shepherd the Church of God which He* [Jesus] *purchased with His own blood"* (Acts 20:28).

When the Scripture says that Christ Jesus died to save sinners, we need to know that His main motivation was not just to save them from hell and make them ready for Heaven, but to make them members of His corporate Body on earth. While Jesus was on earth, His body was the dwelling place and headquarters of God. The body of Jesus was crucified, resurrected, and then seated at the right hand of God in the heavenly places. Jesus then gave the Holy Spirit to the Church. The Holy Spirit was commissioned to birth the Church on the Day of Pentecost. He was then to convict men of sin and draw them to Jesus to become members of the Body of Christ, the Church.

God so loved the world that He gave His Son for its redemption. Jesus so loved the Church that He gave Himself on the cross to purchase the Church with His own blood. He then gave the Holy Spirit to His Church to convict of sin, convert to Christ, empower and enlighten members of the Body of Christ, and to keep purifying and perfecting until it is presented unto Christ a glorious and victorious Church.

GOD THE HOLY SPIRIT'S GIFT

The Holy Spirit's gift to a Christian believer is the divine ability to pray in a supernatural language of the spirit. This divine gift of speaking in an unknown tongue is the divinely given ability to pray in a language that was never learned by natural means. It is an experience received when God baptizes a Christian's redeemed and born-again spirit with the ability to pray in an intelligent language that his or her natural mind did not learn and does not understand or comprehend. It is not a naturally learned ability, but a supernaturally imparted ability. It is not emotional gibberish, meaningless sounds, or hollow expressions. When they receive the gift of the Holy Spirit, many individuals experience great ecstasy in their souls and spirits. The speaking in tongues does not come from being ecstatic, yet it can produce ecstatic feelings, which is the fruit of the Spirit called joy and the zeal of the Lord of Hosts.

The divine spirit language is as real and intelligent as one's learned native language. It is an unknown tongue/language to the one speaking, but it is not unknown to God. It may be a language known and spoken by some of the people on earth, but the majority of the time it is a heavenly language. Apostle Paul used the term "tongues of men and of angels" and declared that when he prayed in tongues his spirit was praying, but his natural mind did not understand or comprehend what was being spoken (see 1 Cor. 13:1; 14:14).

THE GIFT IS FOR ALL BELIEVERS, TILL THE END OF TIME

While Jesus was on earth with His disciples, He declared to them:

> *I will pray the Father, and He will give you another Helper, that He may abide with you forever—the Spirit of truth, whom the world cannot receive, because it neither sees Him*

*nor knows Him; but you know Him, for He dwells with
you and will be in you* (John 14:16-17).

Jesus revealed that He was going to send the Holy Spirit with a
new experience for them: as the Holy Spirit was "with" them now,
He would be "in" them then. Just before Jesus ascended to Heaven
He told the disciples, *"You shall be baptized with the Holy Spirit not
many days from now"* (Acts 1:5).

About 120 of the followers of Jesus went back to Jerusalem
to fulfill the command of Jesus Christ. Jesus commanded them
to wait for the promise of the Father, the baptism with the Holy
Spirit, *"You shall receive power...and you shall be witnesses"* (Acts
1:8). They gathered in an upper room in Jerusalem to wait for the
promise of being baptized with the Holy Spirit. Seven days later,
God's appointed time arrived—in the early morning on the day
the Jews were celebrating the Feast of Pentecost. As the disciples
began praising God that morning, the Holy Spirit suddenly came
like a mighty wind and with tongues of fire that set the believers'
tongues ablaze. They began speaking in unknown tongues as they
received the gift of their spirit languages. They all began to speak
in tongues and continued for quite a while.

After a period of time, Peter stopped speaking in his unknown
tongue and began to preach in their native language of Hebrew to
the multitude of Jews who had gathered to behold and wonder at
what was taking place. Thousands of Jews had gathered at Jerusalem from many nations to celebrate the Feast of Pentecost. Peter
explained to them how the Jews in Jerusalem had crucified Jesus
of Nazareth, who was their promised Messiah. The Jews asked
what they must do to get right with God and receive the wonderful gift that the disciples had received. Peter told them that if
they would repent and be baptized in the name of Jesus Christ for
the remission of sins, they could also receive this gift of the Holy
Spirit. *"For the promise is to you and to your children, and to all who
are afar off"* (Acts 2:39).

Scripture declares that the gift of the Holy Spirit is for every Christian believer during the whole age of the mortal Church. Today we are almost 2,000 years "afar off," but the gift is still for every present-day believer. Jesus and Peter declared that the only conditions to receive the gift of the Holy Spirit were to believe and obey. Jesus proclaimed:

> *He who believes in Me, as the Scripture has said, out of his heart will flow rivers of living water." But this He spoke concerning the Spirit, whom those believing in Him would receive; for the Holy Spirit was not yet given, because Jesus was not yet glorified* (John 7:38-39).

Peter and the other apostles preaching to the Jews stated, *"And we are His witnesses to these things, and so also is the Holy Spirit whom God has given to those who obey Him"* (Acts 5:32).

All 120 followers of Jesus who were gathered together in the upper room on the Day of Pentecost received the Holy Spirit's gift of other tongues—their own spirit languages. It was not just the twelve apostles who received, but all of the other 108 men, women, and young people who were there received the same baptism in the Spirit with the ability to pray in other tongues. The Holy Spirit birthed the New Testament Church that day, which began the dispensation of the Church Age. The 120 became charter members of Christ's newly birthed Church. This established the foundational principle for those who become members of Christ's Church. They are to be born of the Spirit, baptized with water, receive the Holy Spirit gift of their own spirit language, and baptized into the Body of Christ by the Holy Spirit. *"For by one Spirit we are all baptized into the one body"* (1 Cor. 12:13).

THE GREATEST GIFT

SPIRIT-TO-SPIRIT COMMUNICATION

The Bible declares that God is a Spirit. The Holy Spirit's gift of the spirit language enables a person to communicate with God directly from spirit to Spirit—from man's inner spirit being to God who is a Spirit. God formed man's body from the dust of the earth and then breathed His Spirit into him, making man a living soul in a physical body with an eternal spirit. Humans are spirit beings living in natural mortal bodies.

Humans interact with the created world through the five natural senses of seeing, hearing, smelling, tasting, and feeling. They communicate with each other primarily through speaking and listening. Speaking is the unique ability of man that the animal world does not have. Animals can communicate with sounds, but they do not speak in a word language. Man has the ability to learn with his mind and speak with his mouth many different languages.

Those who have been born of the Spirit and baptized with the Spirit receive a spirit language. This gives the believer a private communication line direct to God's throne which cannot be understood or hindered by the devil or natural man. It is like having one's own private telephone to Heaven. However, it is designed to be used for more than communication to God in prayer.

The spirit language is our most powerful power producer. It is one of the greatest ministries to us and to others. It is the greatest gift a Christian can receive, for it is the giver and operator of all the other gifts and graces of God. It will require a whole book to give all the benefits, purposes, and blessings of being gifted with one's own Holy Spirit-given spirit language.

THE TWO GREATEST MIRACLES

God has done—and continues to do—many miracles, but I consider two of His miracles to be superior to the rest. The first of the two greatest miracles is what I call the "father of all miracles." It is greater than God's creation of the whole universe. It is when God transforms a sinner into a saint. God made man as a free moral agent with the power of free will to say "yes" or "no" to God. Humans have the power to yield to God or to oppose God. When God created the heavens and the earth there was no resistance from anywhere. However, when Jesus wants to make a person a new creation being, that person can resist God. Jesus cannot save a person unless he or she yields, believes, and receives Christ into his heart. Therefore, the process that brings about the gift of eternal life in a person is a greater miracle than the creation of Heaven and earth. To activate the gift of eternal life in a man or woman is the father of all miracles.

The "mother of all miracles" is the gift of the Holy Spirit. The Bible declares that the tongue is the most powerful member in the human body. The tongue is so set in the body that it can sanctify the body for God's use or set it on hell's fire for the devil's use. *"But no man can tame the tongue. It is an unruly evil, full of deadly poison"* (James 3:8). No man can tame the tongue, but God can. When God baptizes a person in the Holy Spirit, He tames the tongue by having it speak the language of His Spirit. It takes great faith and trust in God to allow Him to have us speak in a heavenly spirit language that our mind does not understand or know what is being spoken. That is one reason why the Holy Spirit's gift of tongues is the second greatest miracle.

If you have exercised faith to receive the gift of eternal life, then you have experienced the greatest miracle. If you have believed and received the gift of the Holy Spirit by yielding your tongue to speak in unknown tongues, then you have experienced the second greatest miracle. Never let the devil tell you that you do not have faith, for if you have been born again and received your spirit language, then you have exercised your faith for the two greatest miracles in Christianity. Believing God to meet your need for personal divine healing or a miracle is secondary to the two greatest miracles.

By the time you finish reading this book, you will discover how to activate the gifts that are within you. Paul told Timothy, *"Stir up the gift of God which is in you"* (2 Tim. 1:6). The word "activate" is synonymous with "stir up." The gift of eternal life, the gift of the Holy Spirit, and the gifts of the Holy Spirit are within you. In Chapter 6, you will find the four principles for activating any gift of God that is within you. I have trained thousands in prophetic "activations," who have then trained over 250,000 others around the world. These truths and principles are biblical and have proven to work in hundreds of thousands of people.

THE SPIRIT LANGUAGE IS AN ABIDING AND ACTIVE ABILITY

Every Christian needs the gift of the Holy Spirit. If you have received God's gift and Jesus' gift, then you need to receive the Holy Spirit's gift. Let me remind you that God's gift was His Son given for the redemption of the world. Jesus gave the Holy Spirit as a gift to His Church. The Holy Spirit gives all Church members the gift of their own spirit languages when He baptizes them with the Holy Ghost and fire. This was in fulfillment of the prophecy that John the Baptist gave concerning what Jesus would do for His followers: *"He shall baptize you with the Holy Spirit and fire"* (Acts 1:5). *"And they were all filled with the Holy Spirit and began to speak with other tongues as the Spirit gave them utterance"* (Acts 2:4). "Gave them utterance" means that the Holy Spirit gave to their spirits the ability to speak forth in a supernatural spirit language. It was not their learned native tongue but another tongue that was unknown to them. It was a gift given, an abiding ability imparted to their inner spirit being.

This gift becomes a permanent capability and characteristic of the new man in Christ. The inner spirit man can speak at will in his spirit language the same as the natural physical man can speak at will in his native learned language. Man's natural mind and his inner spirit both have access to the mouth for speaking. Apostle Paul said that he could speak at will in his language of the spirit the same as he could speak at will in his learned languages. This is what we want to discover—all the ways we can speak in our spirit language to glorify God, do the works of Christ, and grow to maturity in Christ Jesus.

AN ILLUSTRATION FROM A COMPUTER

Receiving the gift of the Holy Spirit can be compared to the time I received the gift of a computer from my office staff. I could do so much more with it than I could do with my old manual typewriter. When I wrote my first book, *The Eternal Church*,[1] in the late 1970s, I wrote all the material for the nearly 400-page book first in longhand and then typed the material with my manual typewriter. It took me three years to finish the book. When I wrote my tenth book, I finished it in three months with the computer.

However, I have only learned the basic essentials of the computer. I am probably using a mere 10 to 20 percent of its capability. I have not taken the time to be trained in all the ways it could help me write, do research, and communicate. This is an example of most Christians in their use of the gift of the Holy Spirit. Most Spirit-baptized Christians just have the essentials of the gift. They spoke in tongues when they received the gift and they pray in tongues now and then. They are using only 10 percent of all that the gift can do for and through them.

As you read through this book you will discover the other 80 to 90 percent of the valuable benefits, powerful purposes, and miraculous ministries that are available to the Christian who has received the divine ability to pray and minister in his or her spirit language.

70 REASONS CONTINUED...

EIGHTEEN

The spirit language is "the greatest gift" the Holy Spirit could find to give the individual believer. Jesus is the greatest gift God could give for the redemption of the world, and the Holy Spirit is the greatest gift Jesus could give to His Church. Think about it: of all the resources in Heaven, the eternal universe and all of the attributes, gifts, and graces of Almighty God that were available, there was nothing more valuable, beneficial, and important for the Holy Spirit to give to the individual child of God than their own spirit language. It is "the gift" that is the greatest of all for a Spirit-born saint of God (see 1 Cor. 12:31; 14:4).

The spirit language is an intelligent language of our born-of-the-Spirit, new-creation-man in Christ Jesus. It is not emotional gibberish or being ecstatic—although speaking in tongues may produce ecstatic feelings and positive, joyful emotions. The spirit language is the language of one's inner spirit being, as one's learned natural language is the language of one's physical being (see 1 Cor. 14:4; Eph. 3:16; 2 Cor. 4:16).

NINETEEN

Our spirit language enables us to have spirit-to-Spirit communication with God. What an amazing supernatural ability for a mortal human to have! The Word of God declares that God is a Spirit. Humans were created spirit beings clothed with flesh and bone bodies. Man's sin deadened his spirit. Jesus brings the spirit back to life by imparting His everlasting life into the human spirit. The Holy Spirit gives the spirit language to enable us to communicate with God as a spirit being to a Spirit being (see John 4:24; 1 Cor. 15:45; 2 Cor. 3:17; Gen. 2:7; Rom. 5:12; John 3:3-5, 16).

TWENTY

Scripture declares that the gift of the Holy Spirit is for every Christian believer during the whole age of the mortal Church—those at the time of the Early Church "and to all who are afar off." We today are almost 2,000 years "afar off," but the gift is still for every present-day believer (see Acts 2:38-39).

TWENTY-ONE

The spirit language is our most powerful power producer. It is one of the greatest ways to minister to ourselves and others. It is the greatest gift a Christian can receive for it is the giver and operator of all the other gifts and graces of God (see Acts 1:8).

TWENTY-TWO

The "mother of all miracles" is the gift of the Holy Spirit. The Bible teaches that the tongue is the most powerful member in the human body. The tongue is so set in the body that it can sanctify the body for God's use or set it on fire of hell for the devil's use. *Every creature on earth has been tamed by man, but no man can tame the tongue* (James 3:8). No man can tame the tongue, but God can. When God baptizes a person in the Holy Spirit He tames the tongue by having it speak the language of His Spirit. It takes great faith and trust in God to allow Him to have us speak in a heavenly spirit language that our mind does not understand or know what is being spoken. That is one reason why the Holy Spirit's gift of tongues is the second greatest miracle (see James 3:1-12; Prov. 18:21; 1 Cor. 14:2).

TWENTY-THREE

Receiving the gift of the Holy Spirit is like receiving the gift of a computer. The computer has hundreds of programs and capabilities that the person who has previously not had a computer would not know how to use. It takes learning, training, and personal experience to know how to use all of the computer's capabilities. When I first received a computer, I just used it like a typewriter, until I gradually learned other things.

Even after writing three of my ten books on a computer, I just learned how to copy, cut, and paste information from one place to another while writing this chapter! Most tongues-talking Christians use their spirit language like I have used my computer.

Probably 90 percent of Spirit-baptized Christians utilize less than 10 percent of the capabilities and benefits of their spirit language (see Heb. 5:14; Eph. 1:17-18).

ENDNOTE

1. Bill Hamon, *The Eternal Church* (Shippensburg, PA: Destiny Image, 1981, 2003).

CHAPTER 4

TRANSITION FROM THE LAW TO THE CHURCH

THE CHURCH AGE—THE OLD ORDER CEASED, EVERYTHING BECAME NEW!

The age, or dispensation, of the Law began with Moses receiving the Law of God and continued for 1,500 years until Christ Jesus came and ushered in the Church Age. The Church Age continues from the first coming of Christ Jesus until His second coming. Christ's first coming started a new race of humankind with everlasting life in their mortal bodies. At Christ's second coming He will resurrect and translate the bodies of all members of the Church into immortal bodies. That will end the Age of the Mortal Church and begin the Age of the Immortal Church.

When the Immortal Church Age begins, so will the Church-Kingdom race. Members of this race will not only have everlasting life in their spirit-beings, but they will also have everlasting life in their physical beings. Jesus will make their bodies immortal, just as His human body became immortal after it was resurrected from the grave. Everything became new at His first coming, and everything will become new at His second coming.

In the midst of all that happens at His second coming, Jesus declares, *"Behold, I make all things new"* (Rev. 21:5). To make something new means to restore it back to the way it was when it was newly made. Jesus did not say He is going to make all new things; He said He is going to make all things new. The things that exist will be transformed into the original state and glorious way they were in the original creation.

When the Scripture says that Jesus will give us a glorious body like His glorified body, it does not mean a different body but a body like God originally created for humans. The body we lived in on earth will be transformed into a glorious body like the body of Jesus. Christ Jesus did not get a new body from Heaven at His resurrection. The earth body that was crucified on the cross was the same body that was resurrected into an immortal body, ascended into Heaven, and was seated at the right hand of God. This same principle applies when Jesus speaks of a new Heaven and a new earth.

When God establishes a new dispensation or age He also establishes a new order, with new things that did not exist nor operate in the old order. He establishes things that were not available or experienced by the people of the past age or dispensation. This is especially true with the transition from the Law of Moses to the Church of Jesus Christ, from the dispensation of the Law to the dispensation of the Church. Once the new begins, the old ends.

THREE SUCCESSIVE RACES OF HUMANITY

The Church Age started a new race of humankind. Every 2,000 years God has changed His order of humankind's special relationship to Him. First, there was the general human race. In the beginning when God created Adam and Eve, we could call that the year "0." That was the beginning of the human race.

Second, God separated the Israelite race unto Himself. Two thousand years after Adam and Eve, God called Abraham to begin a new race of people in a new place. God gave them a tabernacle, feasts, laws, and the Ten Commandments to demonstrate to the rest of humanity God's ideas of right and wrong and the requirements to approach God for pardon from sins. This race started out being called the Hebrew people. When Jacob had his twelve sons and God changed his name to Israel, they became known as "the children of Israel" or "Israelites." They are also called Jews, after Jacob's son Judah. Today those who live in the nation of Israel are known as "Israelis." But the Israelite race was a special people called out and separated unto God to be His special chosen people.

Third, Jesus, the Son of God, came to earth by human birth approximately 2,000 years after Abraham. At the age of thirty He began demonstrating the Kingdom of God for the next three and one-half years. He then was crucified, buried, resurrected on the third day, ascended back to Heaven, and sat down at the right hand of God. He then sent the Holy Spirit to birth His Church on the Day of Pentecost and thereby began the Church Age. This began the Church race, which was taken from the general human race (Gentiles) and from the Israelite race (Jews). From both Jew and Gentile, God called forth a new people called the Church. The Church became God's chosen people and new race of humankind on planet Earth (see Eph. 2:14-16).

Born-again members of Christ's Church belong to a new race creation in Christ, which is comprised of those who have eternal life in their spirit beings while living in mortal bodies. The rest of the human race—Jews and Gentiles—are declared dead in their trespasses and sins, which means they have eternal death in their spirit beings while living in their mortal bodies. The only way they can be delivered from that death is by having their sins washed away by the blood of Jesus, being born again by the Spirit of God, thereby becoming children of God, citizens of Heaven, and members of the Church race (see Gal. 3:22-29).

A NEW COVENANT FOR A NEW RACE/NATION

The Church Age started God's new covenant with humankind. A covenant is similar to a testament, which is a legal document by which a person declares his will concerning who will receive all his wealth. The Bible is divided into an Old Testament and a New Testament. The New Testament supersedes the Old Testament. The New Testament is the last will and testament of Jesus Christ. A testament and will do not usually become enforced until the death of the testator. The Testator of the New Testament, Jesus the Son of God, died and rose again, thereby making all of His new covenant/testament available to all His heirs. Born-again children of God are heirs of all that God provided through Jesus Christ our Lord and Savior (see Rom. 8:17). Peter declared that the Church race is a new people of God on planet Earth. Those who were not a special people are now the people of God. The Church now becomes God's holy nation on Earth. Israel was God's natural nation with natural people, but the Church is God's spiritual people and spiritual nation, a royal priesthood and a holy nation.

You also, as living stones, are being built up a spiritual house, a holy priesthood, to offer up spiritual sacrifices acceptable to God through Jesus Christ...You are a chosen generation, a royal priesthood, a holy nation, His own special people, that you may proclaim the praises of Him who called you out of darkness into His marvelous light; who once were not a people but are now the people of God (see 1 Pet. 2:5, 9-10).

A TEMPLE FOR GOD'S DWELLING

The Israelite race was commanded to build a temple for God's dwelling place on earth. Moses built the tabernacle, or tent, in the wilderness. Solomon built the temple in Jerusalem. While Jesus was on Earth He revealed to His disciples that He was now the temple of God that was so much greater than the temple Solomon built. He also revealed that He would build a temple for Himself. His temple for His dwelling place would be made from lively stones, which would be the people He would reconcile unto Himself. His new temple would have a new name. This was made known when Jesus made that all important statement, *"I will build My Church!"* (Matt. 16:18).

Christ built the Church as His dwelling place on Earth. Saints are members of the household of God, and we are being fitted together into a building that is growing into a holy temple in the Lord. We are being built together (on earth) for a dwelling place of God in the Spirit (see Eph. 2:19, 21-22). *"Do you not know that your body is the temple of the Holy Spirit?"* (1 Cor. 6:19). The spirits and bodies of Christians are the new temple of God. *"You are the temple of the living God"* (2 Cor. 6:16). All the children of God on earth make up the corporate Body of Christ, which has become God's global temple and His headquarters building on earth. A comprehensive name of the Church is "the one, universal, many-membered, corporate Body of Christ."

EVERYTHING NEW WHEN JESUS CAME

Everything was changed when Jesus became the new way, new life, new truth, and the new and only door to Heaven. Jesus became the one and only Mediator between God and man. All other ways and means of approaching God were removed. No longer could a person join God's people by being born an Israelite. He or she had to be born again to be a child of God. The Church Age changed the name of God's people from "Israelites" to "Christians." A new body was provided—Jesus' body was the dwelling place of God on earth while He was here in His mortal earth body. When Jesus birthed His Church, it became the Body of Christ as Jesus was the body of God. *"For in Him dwells all the fullness of the Godhead bodily"* (Col. 2:9). *"Now you are the body of Christ, and members individually"* (1 Cor. 12:27).

When God established His new nation of the Church, He gave His national people a new language that only citizens of that nation could speak. To become a citizen of the Church nation one must be translated from the kingdom of darkness into the Kingdom of God's dear Son. This is accomplished by a person being born again by the Spirit of God. The Holy Spirit then gifts each person who will believe and receive with his own spirit language.

FROM THE SPEED OF SOUND TO THE SPEED OF LIGHT

The gift of the Holy Spirit increases saints' ability to communicate from the speed of sound to the speed of light. Sandy Catalano, an elder at CI Family Church, was praying in her native language (English) and then switched to her spirit language. Suddenly all the things and people that she had planned to pray for started flashing through her mind faster than the frames of an old movie reel. Sandy thought, Lord, it is going too fast. There is not time enough for me to pray about each one of these requests at this speed. God spoke back to her mind and said, 'That is true when you pray with your natural mind and language, which takes place at the speed of sound. But you are praying with your God-given spirit language, which can pray and communicate at the speed of light.'

That brought new revelation and understanding of the power of praying in tongues. God is Light and His Spirit is light. When we pray with our spirit language we connect with God and function in His dimension of light. More can be accomplished in minutes of praying in the spirit than can be accomplished in hours of praying with our limited natural knowledge and abilities. This is just one of the many advantages and benefits of receiving and using one's gift of the Holy Spirit.

70 REASONS CONTINUED...

TWENTY-FOUR

When God established His new nation of the Church, He gave His national people a new language that only citizens of that nation could speak. To become a citizen of the Church nation one must be translated from the kingdom of darkness into the Kingdom of God's dear Son. This is accomplished by a person being born again by the Spirit of God. The Holy Spirit then gifts each one, who will believe and receive, with his own spirit language, which become his identifying national language (see Col. 1:13; John 3:3; 1 Pet. 2:9; Heb. 12:22).

TWENTY-FIVE

When we pray with our natural mind and language, our praying takes place at the speed of sound, but when we pray with our God-given spirit language, we pray and communicate at the speed of light. This is new revelation and understanding of the power of praying in tongues. It works that way because God is light and His Spirit is light. We are children of light and we are to live and walk in the light. When we pray with our spirit languages we connect with God and function in His dimension of light. More can be accomplished in minutes of praying in the spirit than can be accomplished in hours of praying with our limited natural knowledge and ability (see John 8:12; 9:5; 12:36; 1 John 1:5, 7; 1 Thess. 5:5).

CHAPTER 5

A POWER-PRODUCING PLANT

Jesus declared to His followers, *"But you shall receive power when the Holy Spirit has come upon you; and you shall be witnesses to Me in Jerusalem, and in all Judea and Samaria, and to the end of the earth"* (Acts 1:8). Peter gave the following instructions in his preaching on the Day of Pentecost, when the people inquired what they must do to be saved and receive the gift of the Holy Spirit like the disciples had received:

> *Now when they heard this, they were cut to the heart, and said to Peter and the rest of the apostles, "Men and brethren, what shall we do?" Then Peter said to them, "Repent, and let every one of you be baptized in the name of Jesus Christ for the remission of sins; and you shall receive the gift of the Holy Spirit"* (Acts 2:37-38).

Peter told them they had to receive Jesus Christ as their Savior and be baptized into His name, and then they would become qualified candidates to receive the gift of the Holy Spirit. They had to obey this command to receive the Holy Spirit.

"And we are His witnesses to these things, and so also is the Holy Spirit whom God has given to them who obey Him" (Acts 5:32).

Those who saw Christ ascend were commanded *"not to depart from Jerusalem, but to wait for the Promise of the Father"* (Acts 1:4) with the assurance of Jesus Christ that *"you shall be baptized with the Holy Spirit not many days from now."* For *"you shall receive power when the Holy Spirit has come upon you"* (Acts 1:4-5, 8). After they had received the gift of the Holy Spirit they would have the divine ability to produce the power of God within and through their lives.

ILLUSTRATION OF AN ELECTRICAL POWER PLANT

The greatest illustration of the power of the Holy Spirit in our lives that I have found in my fifty-eight years of ministry and sixty years of being a born-again, Holy Spirit-baptized Christian is how electrical power is produced. Electricity is produced by water flowing through the water gate of a dam. Within the water gate is a turbine which is defined as "any of a class of engines which deliver power created by a continuous flow or jets of steam, air, water or other liquids, against the curved blades or vanes of a rotor or series of rotors."[1] In this illustration we are interested in the flow of water against the curved blades of a turbine.

The water gate is opened to allow the water from the river that has been formed into a reservoir of water to flow over the turbine causing it to turn at tremendous speeds. The turbine produces the power to turn a great dynamo in the heart of the dam. The dynamos produce the electrical power. The definition of a dynamo is an "electric machine that converts energy from a mechanical into an electrical form by the use of electromagnets; a generator."[2]

I developed and started using this illustration in 1958 when my wife and I took a tour of Hoover Dam, which is built on the Colorado River about thirty miles east of Las Vegas, Nevada. The dam across the river produced Lake Mead, which is the backed-up river water that flows through the turbines of the dam. It produces much of the electricity for several of the western states in America.

Let us now look at the elements in the operation of a dam and how this process produces powerful electricity. We will then show how the spiritual application of this reveals our own built-in power plant that can produce the supernatural power of God in and through our lives.

NATURAL ELEMENTS WITH SPIRITUAL APPLICATION

River and Reservoir of Water—Filled with the Holy Spirit

» Water Gate—Mouth of the Believer

» Turbine—Tongue of the Believer

» Dynamo—Man's spirit and the Holy Spirit are one

» Transformer—Wisdom to distribute the power

» Fuse/Switch—On=Faith, Off=Unbelief, Blown=Fear

THE RIVER AND RESERVOIR OF WATER

When a dam is built on a river, it causes the water to back up and form a reservoir, such as Lake Mead. The reservoir water on its side of the dam is the same water that eventually flows through the turbine and continues on as a river. However, in the process of producing power, the water becomes much more active, noisy, and turbulent as it goes through the turbines.

The reservoir of water is typical of a person who has been born of the Spirit and is full of the Spirit of God but has never received the Holy Spirit's gift. We could say that the water on the reservoir side of the dam is more typical of evangelical Christianity. The water is more tranquil, orderly, and deep. It is good for catching fish, which is evangelism. It is good for water baptisms. Its waters can be used for cleansing, which is typical of sanctification and holiness. The reservoir is great for boating, which represents what we call fellowshipping. Nevertheless, the water upstream from the dam does not produce supernatural power. It has to go through the water gate and turn the turbine to produce power.

The Charismatic viewpoint of a person being Spirit-filled is different than that of Evangelicals. Charismatics think of being Spirit-filled to the extent of overflowing with speaking in tongues. As we have seen, the gift of the Holy Spirit is the divine ability given to believers to pray in a new spiritual language. Praying in one's spirit language is like the river flowing, which activates one's spiritual turbine. The activation of the turbine is what starts the chain reaction that produces the power that empowers things to work.

THE WATER GATE

The water gate is representative of the mouth of a Christian. God says to His people, *"Open your mouth wide, and I will fill it"* (Ps. 81:10). Our gates and doors must be open for Christ to come into us and to flow out of us. Jesus said, *"If anyone hears My voice and opens the door, I will come in to him and dine with him, and he with Me"* (Rev. 3:20).

God established a divine principle that requires an act of faith on man's part for God to relate to him. Jesus declared this principle several times in the Gospels. He continually spoke about people asking, seeking, knocking, confessing, speaking, and believing in order to receive Him and demonstrate His works. Christians must ask for the gift of the Holy Spirit, believe in their heart, open their mouths, and begin to speak in other tongues as the Spirit divinely enables in order to fully receive and have the gift of the Holy Spirit. Every gift and blessing from God is received and manifested the same way, whether it is the initial supernatural gift of eternal life or the powerful gifts of the Holy Spirit.

"Lift up your heads, O you gates! And be lifted up, you everlasting doors! And the King of glory shall come in" (Ps. 24:7). In ancient times the gate of a city was what was opened to let people in and out of the city. In the natural the mouth is the gate to the stomach, but spiritually it is the gate to the soul. It is with our mouths that we confess the Lord Jesus Christ allowing Him to come into our hearts. It is with our mouths that we exercise our faith to accomplish great things for God. For with the heart man believes unto righteousness, but it is with the mouth that man makes confession unto salvation. Apostle Paul declared that the word of faith that he preached was in the hearts and mouths of the saints (see Rom. 10:8-10).

God made humankind in His own likeness and image. Of all God's creation on Earth, man is the only one with the power of speech. All of God's other creatures on earth have their different ways of communicating with each other, but man is the only species that speaks with such a vocabulary of words. Speaking words is the main method of communication in the human race. Some people can speak several learned languages. God speaks and so He gave His masterpiece creation the ability to speak. God wanted to speak to humankind and He wanted humankind to speak to Him.

FROM PROOF TO PROVISION

God chose believers speaking by their divinely enabled spirits in an unlearned language as the evidence that they had received the gift of the Holy Spirit. Speaking with our spirit in a language unknown to us is proof that we have received the gift of the Holy Spirit, for the Holy Spirit's gift to a believer is receiving one's own unknown tongue-spirit language. But it was given for much more than evidence of a person being baptized with the Holy Spirit.

This special gift/grace of God's unmerited divine enablement to speak in our spirit language goes from proof to provision.

Speaking in tongues provides the believer with many ways to access and activate the attributes of God. Our initial gifted ability to pray from our spirit in an unlearned language is just the entry into God's storehouse of wisdom, power, revelation, and supernatural ministry. Once we enter by this doorway into spiritual ministry, there are many rooms in God's mansion that reveal and release the different purposes and benefits for speaking in tongues. The main point here is that you must open the gate of your mouth in order to receive and derive all the benefits of speaking with your spirit language.

THE TURBINE—TONGUE OF THE BELIEVER

The Bible gives much importance to the tongue. The capability and power of the tongue is most vividly portrayed with many explanations and illustrations in James 3:2-8:

> *If anyone can control his tongue, it proves that he has perfect control over himself in every other way. We can make a large horse turn around and go wherever we want by means of a small bit in his mouth. And a tiny rudder makes a huge ship turn wherever the pilot wants it to go, even though the winds are strong.*

> *So also the tongue is a small thing, what enormous damage it can do. A great forest can be set on fire by one tiny spark. And the tongue is a flame of fire. It is full of wickedness, and poisons every part of the body. And the tongue is set on fire by hell itself, and can turn our whole lives into a blazing flame of destruction and disaster.*

> *Men have trained, or can train, every kind of animal or bird that lives and every kind of reptile and fish, but no human being can tame the tongue* (TLB).

Verse two declares that if a man does not allow his tongue to speak wrong words at the wrong place and time, he is a mature person. If an individual can control his tongue he (or she) can control his whole body. The tongue is like a little match that can set a whole forest on fire. It is like the bridle bits put in a horse's mouth that can turn his body any way the rider wants him to go. It is like the rudder on a ship or steering wheel of a car, which can determine the direction the vessel goes. Verse six says that though the tongue is a little member it can influence the whole body. In fact, it says that *"The tongue is so set among our members that it defiles the whole body, and sets on fire the course of nature; and it is set on fire by hell."* This implies that God put the tongue at the right place in the body with the power to affect the body, soul, and spirit in certain ways.

The main way the tongue affects matters is by speaking words. Proverbs 18:21 declares that words have the power of life and death. The tongue of the wise is health and a wholesome tongue is a tree of life (see Prov. 12:18; 15:4). Jesus said the words He spoke were spirit and life (see John 6:63). And by the words we speak with our tongues we will be justified and by the words we speak we will be condemned (see Matt. 12:37). God created the earth and everything on it by His words. He spoke all of creation into existence (except humankind). When one prays in tongues it is not nonsensical sounds, but intelligent words of a real language. They are words directed by the Spirit of God.

Scientists and theologians may not know all the ways this works, but the God who made every detail and operation of man knows fully the purpose and power of the tongue He made within the human body. Jesus had many reasons for choosing to give His believers the gifted ability to pray with words that are inspired by the Holy Spirit like the words He spoke. The Word of God declares emphatically that natural words spoken by our tongues can have a negative or positive effect upon our bodies. Likewise, when we speak spiritual words with our spirit language it similarly affects our spirit and soul. By the time you have finished reading this book you will discover and understand the numerous ways this is accomplished.

When the tongue is controlled by evil it can defile the whole body. Since a tongue motivated by evil can defile the whole body, then when a tongue is motivated to speak by the righteous Holy Spirit it can sanctify the whole body. When we use our tongues to speak in our spirit language it activates our supernatural new creation nature and sets us aflame with heavenly passion. James 3:7-8 declares that every kind of creature on earth has been tamed by man, but no man can tame the tongue. That is another reason Jesus chose believers speaking in unknown tongues as the demonstration that they have been baptized with the Holy Spirit: it demonstrates that though no man can tame the tongue, yet Jesus by His Spirit can control and direct the human tongue (see Matt. 15:11-18).

In our illustration of the electrical power plant, the tongue is like the turbine placed in a gate of the great wall of a dam. The opening of the gate and the turning of the turbine from the river of water flowing through it determines the amount of electrical power that is produced. There is no power produced until the water flows through the turbine. The water flowing through the turbine is typical of speaking in tongues. The water must come from the depths of the reservoir of water and flow through the turbine to produce power.

We must allow the Holy Spirit, who is in the depth of the reservoirs of our spirit, to flow through our tongues in our spirit language to produce the power of God in our lives. Jesus declared to His followers that they would receive this experience and have this power-producing ability when He baptized them with His Spirit:

"He who believes in Me, as the Scripture has said, out of his heart will flow rivers of living water." But this He spoke concerning the Spirit, whom those believing in Him would receive; for the Holy Spirit was not yet given, because Jesus was not yet glorified (John 7:38-39).

But you shall receive power when the Holy Spirit has come upon you... (Acts 1:8).

Notice that Jesus declared that when believers receive the gift of the Holy Spirit, the reservoirs of their spirits are filled with God's life-giving water. The Holy Spirit gift of other tongues gives the ability for that water to flow out of the reservoirs of our hearts into the water gates of our mouths and through the turbines of our tongues, thereby activating the power-producing plant within us. A Christian does not automatically have the power Jesus spoke of just because the reservoir of his heart has been filled with Holy Spirit water. The statements Jesus made imply that we receive the power when we open the water gate and allow the water to move the turbine. It is when the living water flows out that it produces power within and activates God's power to flow through us.

A MILLION-DOLLAR EXAMPLE

Another way to understand the gift of the spiritual language is to imagine that Jesus had someone deposit one million dollars into your bank account. Your bank account is filled with money, but it does not do you any good—or anyone else—unless you write checks on it and purchase something. Knowing your bank account is full may give you some joy and comfort, but it is not fulfilling the purpose of having the money in your account.

Many Christians rejoice and are comforted knowing that they have received the Holy Spirit's gift. But they are not writing any checks on their accounts, nor are they allowing any money to flow out so that they can produce profitable things for themselves and others. Money is put into our accounts to give us power to purchase. Jesus places the Holy Spirit power within us to fully manifest His life and demonstrate His Kingdom.

Some only write checks for small amounts—just enough to survive. God does not want His children to have a minimal, survival-only mentality. We need to ask ourselves, "Why am I not writing bigger checks on my heavenly bank account?" God's million dollar deposit is not a once-in-a-lifetime deposit; He will continually keep the account filled if we will use the account for His Kingdom purposes.

Scientists have discovered that the most intelligent human beings have used less than 10 percent of their brain power. Christians are probably using less than 10 percent of the power of God that is within them. Does God want us to use the other 90 percent? If so, how can we access it and activate that power? What we are covering in this book will reveal some of the ways that Christians can increase their percentage. If a person put into practice the truths discovered here and only increased their spiritual output by 10 percent, they would still be doing double what most Christians are doing. That would be one way of receiving the double portion that many of us desire to receive.

THE CURRENCY OF HEAVEN AND EARTH

Money is the medium of exchange for all earthly things. A word of faith spoken with Holy Spirit power is the medium of exchange for all heavenly things. Speaking in tongues is the key to our victory, because faith is the victory that overcomes. Faith is the currency of Heaven as money is the currency of earth. If a person has enough money he can purchase anything that man has to offer. If a person has enough faith, he can procure all that Heaven has to offer. Jesus put no limitations on the possibilities of what faith can procure. Jesus said, *"If you can believe, all things are possible"* (Mark 9:23). Apostle Paul revealed that *"God is able to do exceedingly abundantly above all that we ask or think, according to the power that works in us"* (Eph. 3:20).

Jude 1:20 declares that praying in tongues generates faith in an individual. *"Beloved, Build yourselves upon your most holy faith by praying in the Holy Spirit."* It charges a believer's spirit and builds him up in his most holy faith. This spiritual power is produced like powerful electricity is produced at a dam. The water flowing out of the water gate through the turbine turns the big dynamos which generate electrical power. The more we pray in our spirit language the more we charge our spirit with faith and power. God is able to do all things in us and through us, but how much can be done is according to the amount of faith and power we have within us. The more ways we can find to increase God's faith and power within us the more powerful and productive we can be in our lives and ministries.

To increase our faith we must know what produces faith, its area of operation and what activates it. The location and operation of faith is in the heart and mouth. The word of faith is in your heart and mouth—with your heart you believe it and with your mouth you speak it. Therefore, speaking, whether in our native tongue or an unknown tongue, is the determining factor in our victorious living. That's why the book of Jude tells Christians to build up themselves in the most holy faith by praying in the Holy Spirit with their spirit prayer languages.

Let us now examine the dynamo and see its application to the Christian spiritual life.

THE DYNAMO—OUR INNER SPIRIT BEING ONE WITH THE HOLY SPIRIT

The dynamo is located down in the heart of the dam. It is like a giant generator. The dynamo is the machine that generates electricity by rotating conducting coils in a magnetic field.

Prophet Ezekiel saw a vision of four wheels and all four had the same likeness. The appearance of their workings was, as it were, a wheel in the middle of a wheel. Wherever the spirit wanted to go the wheels went, for the spirit of the living creatures was in the wheels (see Ezek. 1:16-21). A dynamo is like a wheel turning in the middle of a wheel. And wherever the language of the spirit wants to go the dynamo goes, for the Spirit of the Creator is in the dynamo. Ezekiel saw a vision of the wheel in the middle of a wheel, but we have the spiritual wheel in the middle of a wheel in us, our spirit dynamo.

The dynamo is typical of the redeemed human spirit that has been made one with the Holy Spirit. When we are born of the Spirit and then baptized with the Holy Spirit He becomes one with our spirit and makes our bodies His body.

Do you not know that your bodies are members of Christ?... He who is joined to the Lord is one spirit with Him....Do you not know that your body is the temple of the Holy Spirit who is in you, whom you have from God, and you are not your own? For you were bought at a price; therefore glorify God in your body and in your spirit, which are God's (see 1 Cor. 6:15, 17, 19-20).

Our redeemed spirit, saturated with the Holy Spirit, is the dynamo within our being where all of Christ's gifts, graces, power, and attributes are generated within and through us. The dynamo is activated and maintained by the turning of the turbine. The more the turbine operates the more power the dynamo generates.

I received a good illustration of this process after I moved the headquarters of Christian International Ministries Network from Arizona to the panhandle of Florida in 1984. We purchased twenty acres of land, which included seventeen acres of forest and two swampy ponds. So we bought a big 1952 Caterpillar™ bulldozer to clear the forest and to make the two swamps into ponds. It had a gigantic diesel engine with big pistons that gave power to perform. A battery was not powerful enough to start that big engine. It would have taken many batteries combined together, but there was not enough space available to place that many batteries on the Caterpillar™.

So the builders put a smaller motor on the big machine. It was a little larger than a lawnmower motor. When we wanted to start the big Caterpillar™ we had to first start the smaller motor. It was called a "pony motor" because it was used to activate the horse power of the big engine—in fact we had to pull a rope to start the pony motor. We would start the pony motor and rev it up to a fast speed and then pull the big lever that engaged the big engine. The pistons that had been cold and idle would start moving with smoke billowing out of the exhaust pipe. When the engine was warmed up with all pistons moving in rhythmic power, we could then use the machine to accomplish all we needed to do to prepare our land for habitation.

Our spirit language is our pony motor that activates the powerful gifts of the Holy Spirit. Every mighty minister with a miracle-working ministry whom I have spoken with during my fifty-eight years of ministry said that he (or she) prays for hours in tongues in the afternoon before he goes to an evening meeting to minister miracles to the people.

AN EXAMPLE OF PROPHESYING

I can give a personal testimony to how this works. Prophecy is one of the gifts of the Holy Spirit. I started manifesting this gift in 1953. Most of the time, it was general congregational prophesying or prophesying with other ministers in prophetic presbytery. But in 1973 God sovereignly released me into a greater dimension of prophetic ministry. During the previous twenty years I gave personal prophecies to no more than fifteen people at one setting. But when God activated me into that new anointing, I prophesied at times over hundreds of people during one service. It was an endless flow of the river of prophetic utterance.

To continue prophesying hour after hour, I had to keep my spirit charged up by praying in tongues in between prophesying to people. Usually I would speak in tongues for a while before starting to prophesy. A woman spoke to me saying, "If you did not spend time praying in tongues you could have time to prophesy over more people." I explained to her that when I first start prophesying and also when I get physically weary I need to run my pony motor for a while to give me power to get the big piston engine of prophesying moving with power.

ACTIVATE YOUR PONY MOTOR

Praying in our spirit language has the power to activate the gifts of the Spirit that are within us. Our spirit is like the battery that does not have the power to activate the gifts of the Spirit, but our spirit empowered by the pony motor of talking in tongues has the power to activate and manifest the supernatural gifts of the Holy Spirit. Our redeemed human spirit must believe and our mouth and hands must take action to speak and lay hands on people.

Hardly any Christians manifest the miraculous spiritual gifts without first receiving the gift of the Holy Spirit. However, unbelievable as it is, most of the 600 million Christians who have received the Holy Spirit's gift of their own spirit languages do not manifest the supernatural gifts of the Holy Spirit. Why is this? There are several reasons. Christians do not have a good understanding of the power and purpose of speaking in tongues. They do not use speaking in tongues all the ways God intended. There is a lack of revelation of the power and authority the Holy Spirit brings when He baptizes a believer. Saints do not use the tools God gave them to access and activate the power of God. We must come to believe that we have what God says we have and that we can do what God's Word says we can do. Jesus said that those who believe can do the works that He did. Faith in God works—whether one talks in tongues or not. However, the Bible declares that we build up ourselves in the most holy faith by praying in the Holy Spirit/tongues (see Jude 1:20).

We have all the spiritual equipment for producing the power of God as illustrated in the way a dam with its equipment produces electrical power with its water, turbines, and dynamos.

The turbine turning in the water gate works with the dynamo like the pony motor did with the powerful Caterpillar™ engine. The dynamo produces the power, but it takes the turbines to get it started. After it is going the turbines are used as needed to keep the dynamo operating. Jesus gave us speaking in tongues to be our turbine to activate our dynamo within, which is our redeemed and baptized spirit. These are all parts and functions of our own built-in power plant. We are not dependent upon outside sources and circumstances. We have the ability to activate and generate the attributes, presence, and power of God anytime we open the water gate and let the water turn our turbine. This activates our dynamo to generate any attribute of the Holy Spirit that we need. Yes, talking in tongues with our spirit language is one of the main keys that Jesus said He would give that opens the Kingdom of God to us (see Matt. 16:19).

CONVERSION FROM NATURAL TO SPIRITUAL

There is a very important and relevant truth found in the definition of a dynamo: "A dynamo is an electric machine that converts energy from a mechanical into an electrical form."[3] The operation of the dynamo takes the mechanical operation of the turbine and converts it into powerful electricity. A natural operation that can be seen and heard activates an invisible powerful force that can be carried on electrical lines. This electrical power can be used for numerous things.

The process of talking in a language we do not understand sometimes feels like so much mechanical activity. But praying in our spirit language is never useless or a waste of our time. For talking in tongues activates our dynamo-spirit within the heart of our being which converts our mechanical talking-in-tongues energy from a natural form into a spiritual, supernatural power form that can be used for powerful works. Our mouth and hands are like the electrical lines for carrying the power of God to others. That power enables us to fulfill Christ's command for us to lay hands on the sick and heal them and to speak the powerful words of life that transform lives. Talking in tongues at times may seem mechanical and only natural, but it is still doing its work of activating our inner spirit to be personally charged with power to bless and minister the works of Christ to others.

DYNAMO GENERATES *DUNAMIS*

Jesus said that His believers would receive power when they were baptized with the Holy Spirit. The Greek word for the English word "power" is *dunamis*: "It denotes inherent ability, capability, ability to perform anything."[4] When *dunamis* is translated as "ability" it means:

> The power or ability residing in a person; it is power in action, e.g., when put forth in performing miracles; it is sometimes used of the miracle or sign itself. It occurs 118 times in the New Testament. *Dunamis* is also translated as abundance, deed, might, power, strength, violence, virtue, and work.[5]

Using our power-producing plant illustration, Jesus was saying that when we receive our turbine we also receive our dynamo. You shall receive power (*dunamis*, dynamo) when you receive your other tongues (turbine, ability to pray with your spirit language).

I have spoken with and interviewed some of the best-known ministers who manifest the miraculous in their ministries, such as Oral Roberts, Benny Hinn, Reinhard Bonnke, and Guillermo Maldonado. Most of them state that they spend hours praying in tongues before they go to a meeting where they plan to preach and release the miraculous. They do this for two main reasons: to charge themselves with the power of God, which is generated into their beings as they pray in tongues; and to wait on the Lord while praying in tongues to receive words of knowledge and wisdom concerning what the Holy Spirit wants them to do.

I have been a co-speaker with Guillermo in several large meetings. He feels one of the keys God has given him for faith to perform miracles is to hear a word from the Lord concerning what needs Jesus wants to meet first. Praying in tongues turns the light of revelation on in our minds, enabling us to hear the voice of God and see what Christ wants to do in a meeting. When you know you are doing what Christ Jesus wants to do in that service, it activates your faith and gives confidence that all you have to do is be an instrument in the hand of God for Him to accomplish His works.

THE GOSPEL OF THE KINGDOM WILL BE PREACHED

As Christians receive revelation on how to properly use their spirit languages and increase their faith in God and His Holy Spirit power within them, then we will begin to see the miraculous power of God manifest throughout the world. My passion is to see every Christian manifesting Christ Jesus in the fullness of His life and power. Then the world will see Jesus Christ as the only true and Almighty Savior and God. They will proclaim that no religion, philosophy, or so-called god is like Jehovah God and His Son Jesus Christ. As saints manifest the supernatural and demonstrate the Kingdom of God, it will cause the glory of God to fill the earth as the waters cover the sea (see Hab. 2:14). It will cause the greatest revival and harvest of souls ever recorded in Church history.

Jesus said the end could not come and His return could not take place until the gospel of the Kingdom was preached in all the world for a witness (see Matt. 24:14). The gospel of the Kingdom is more than the gospel of salvation. The gospel of salvation is the proclamation of the death, burial, and resurrection of Jesus Christ. The gospel of the Kingdom is the demonstration of the Lordship of Jesus Christ over sin, sickness, demons, people, and nations. Most of Jesus' ministry was comprised of preaching and demonstrating the Gospel of the Kingdom which includes declaring and demonstrating that the kingdoms of this world are all destined to become the kingdoms of our Lord Jesus Christ and His anointed one the Church (see Rev. 11:15).

THE TRANSFORMER—WISDOM TO DISTRIBUTE THE POWER

The definition of a transformer is: "An appliance in alternating current circuits for changing high voltage current to a lower voltage, or low voltage current to a higher voltage. A device that changes AC voltage. Also called a power adapter."[6]

A transformer can take a flow of thousands of volts of electricity from the electrical plant to a city or a community that has need of power. A smaller transformer will reduce the voltage down to 220 and 110 volts as it goes to the individual houses. The Holy Spirit flows from God with millions of volts of God's power. But individuals are not capable of receiving and distributing that much power. The Holy Spirit is the main transformer that distributes the supernatural gifts to individual saints according to their capacity to receive and manifest. Every Spirit-filled saint is given a portion of the work of the Holy Spirit to manifest.

Apostle Paul took three chapters (12, 13, and 14) in his first letter to the Corinthian church to explain the flow/current of the Holy Spirit. These chapters could be called God's main transformer/wisdom for the control, direction, and use of the personal gift of tongues and the corporate use of the gifts of the Holy Spirit. Gifts are distributed to individual believers according to the wisdom and will of the Holy Spirit. Gifts and talents are given on the individual's capability of using, manifesting, and ministering the gift (see Matt. 25:15).

DIVERSITIES OF GIFTS

The following selected Scriptures in First Corinthians 12:1-11 describe the operation of the gifts of the Holy Spirit. *"Spiritual gifts"* and *"manifestations of the Spirit"* are terms expressing this same operation.

Now concerning spiritual gifts, brethren, I do not want you to be ignorant....There are diversities of gifts, but the same Spirit... But the manifestation of the Spirit is given to each one for the profit of all: for to one is given the word of wisdom through the Spirit, to another the word of knowledge through the same Spirit, to another faith by the same Spirit, to another gifts of healings by the same Spirit, to another the working of miracles, to another prophecy, to another discerning of spirits, to another different kinds of tongues, to another the interpretation of tongues. But one and the same Spirit works all these things, distributing to each one individually as He wills.

Notice that the last statement declares that this is a work of the Holy Spirit and He determines the capacity of each individual saint. Then according to His wisdom and will He distributes one or more of the gifts to each member of the Body of Christ. Jesus conveyed this truth in His parable of the talents. *"A man...called his own servants and delivered his goods to them. And to one he gave five talents, to another two, and to another one, to each according to his own ability"* (Matt. 25:14-15). Notice that the talents were given according to the ability of the servants. The Holy Spirit is the only one who knows whether we have the ability to manifest one, two, or five gifts of the Spirit. He is the transformer who determines how much power comes to our houses.

Some translations call the nine gifts in First Corinthians 12 the nine graces of the Spirit. That works as long as one has a complete understanding of divine grace. Grace is God's unmerited, supernatural divine enablement. Whether we call them gifts, graces, or manifestations, they are divine enablements freely given by the will and wisdom of the Holy Spirit.

There are several important truths revealed in these three chapters of First Corinthians. Christians are not to be ignorant (lacking a workable knowledge) concerning spiritual gifts. Most of Christendom is ignorant concerning the existence and operation of spiritual gifts. And the majority of Spirit-filled, tongue-talking Christians do not have a workable knowledge of the gifts of the Holy Spirit. The gifts of the Spirit were given to the Church and they were to be manifested during the whole Church Age. These nine gifts mentioned here reveal the nature of God just as the nine attributes called the fruit of the Spirit do (see Gal. 5:22-23).

For instance, the nine gifts of the Spirit can be placed in three categories containing three gifts each. Diversity of tongues, interpretation of tongues, and prophecy are categorized as the vocal gifts. Word of knowledge, word of wisdom, and discerning of spirits are the revelation gifts. Gifts of healings, the gift of faith, and working of miracles are the power gifts. The nine gifts reveal that God's nature is to talk, to reveal, and to demonstrate His mighty power. It is God's eternal nature to communicate by verbal expression. He will be forever revealing to His people more of Himself and His wonderful works. And the Almighty God will continue to display His power throughout eternity. The gifts reveal and demonstrate the nature and attributes of Jesus Christ. They are

God's love in action. It is good to tell a sick person, "I love you and am sorry you are sick," but it is better to say, "I love you, and in the name of Jesus Christ be healed!" I would much rather have someone's healing faith rather than their words of loving sympathy.

USE THEM OR LOSE THEM

We are to have a workable knowledge of the gifts. Every Spirit-filled saint has one or more gifts to minister the life of Christ to others. It is not as important which gift we have as it is how faithful we are to use the gift and fulfill Christ's purpose for giving us that divine ability. To receive a gift and then not use it is no light matter with the Lord. The person who received only one talent/gift but refused to use it did not receive the commendation of "well done, good and faithful servant." Rather the master called him a wicked and slothful servant. He took the one talent he had and gave it to the man who used his five and doubled them to ten. Then Jesus established the divine principle that those who use what they are given will receive more, but those who will not use their gifts will have them taken from them and given to another. This is where I developed the statement concerning the gifts we receive, "Use them or lose them."

For thirty years we have conducted seminars and schools of the Holy Spirit where we teach and activate saints in their gifts of the Holy Spirit. I teach on the principle that if you do not use your gift, then God will take it from you and give it to those who are using their gifts. I then challenge the attendees with these statements: "I want to make an agreement with you that if you are not going to use your gifts to bless others, then when you leave here to go home your gifts stay with me and my staff." They kind of laugh, but it drives home the fact of saints being serious about stirring up their gifts by being activated and trained to use their weapons of warfare against the enemy and to meet the needs of God's people.

The Scriptures say to "desire spiritual gifts" and "stir up the gift of God which is in you" and "as each one has received a gift, minister it to one another as good stewards of the manifold grace of God" (see 1 Cor. 14:1,12, 39; 2 Tim. 1:6; 1 Pet. 4:10). I remind people who are unwilling to fulfill these commands of what Jesus said to the lazy, fearful servant who would not use his talents, *"Cast the unprofitable servant into the outer darkness* [where] *there will be weeping and gnashing of teeth"* (Matt. 25:30). I do not fully know what all that means, but I don't want to find out by experience!

THE MOTIVATION CAN BE LOVE OR FEAR

If a saint cannot be motivated out of love and desire, then I try to motivate them with a reverential fear of God. Hebrews 2:3-4 declares, *"how shall we escape if we neglect so great a salvation, which at the first began to be spoken by the Lord, and was confirmed to us by those who heard Him, God also bearing witness both with signs and wonders, with various miracles, and gifts of the Holy Spirit"* [the gifts of the Holy Spirit are part of our "great salvation"]. Everyone is motivated by fear of loss or hope of gain. If a saint cannot be motivated by the hope of gaining the reward for faithful obedience, then he must be motivated by the fear of loss that comes with fearful disobedience. Be motivated by the love or fear of God, but be motivated to use your gift. The consequences of being ignorant of spiritual gifts and not using one's spiritual gifts are very serious and costly.

What motivates a person to make the right choice is not as relevant as the fact they took the right action. It is like being motivated to receive the gift of eternal life. I was mainly motivated to get saved, not from a great love for God, but by the fear of hell. That is what got me started serving God, but for decades now I have served God because of my love and appreciation for Jesus Christ. Now, after more than half a century of serving God, I am convinced that Jesus Christ is the only way to be, the only truth to believe, and the only life to live. I have the hope of gaining Heaven and missing hell, but if there was no hell to escape from or Heaven to gain, the life of Jesus is still the only life I want to live both now and forevermore.

It is not as important how we are motivated as it is for us to be motivated to do the will of God. It is the will of God for every Spirit-filled Christian to manifest the gifts of the Spirit.

There are many more points that we could cover, but the main point in this illustration is that the Holy Spirit is the transformer that determines how many gifts we receive and how much power comes into our house.

THE FUSE/SWITCH

On=Faith, Off=Unbelief, Blown=Fear

The definition of fuse is: "A safety device consisting of a strip of wire that melts or breaks an electric circuit if the current exceeds a safe level."[7]

The definition of switch is: "A device for making (switch on) and breaking (switch off) an electrical connection."[8] Every electrical operation has a switch for turning the flow of the electrical current on and off. At big electrical plants switches are gigantic levers, but in a house or business they are little plastic switches. For the lights to come on in a house the switch has to be turned on. There can be more than enough power coming to a plant, business, or house to operate all its machines and appliances; however, if the switch is not turned on, nothing operates.

Faith is our spiritual switch. But a person has to know where the switch is located and how to operate it. The Bible declares that the location of faith is in our hearts and mouths (see Rom. 10:8-10). Faith is the switch that connects and activates the power of God to flow through us to do the works of Christ. If we do not believe that we are who Christ Jesus says we are and that we can do what Jesus says we can do, then we cannot turn on the switch of faith. Faith comes from hearing a *rhema* word from God. When we receive revelation and inspiration from the Spirit we know the switch is fully connected to the power. We then have faith to turn the switch on to start operating things. Faith turns the power on.

Unbelief keeps the switch off, not allowing the power to operate things. The Bible says that the children of Israel could not possess their promised Canaan land because of unbelief. In that land was the abundance of all that they would ever need. However, because of unbelief, they would not turn the switch on so that power would be available to take the abundance of the wealth of Canaan. Faith is the switch that activates and operates (see Heb. 3:18–4:1).

The gifts of the Spirit are sovereignly given by the will and choice of the Holy Spirit, but they are activated and operated by faith. The Holy Spirit brings the power up to the switch of faith, but if faith is not activated—that is, if no one takes action—then no power is manifested. One of the gifts/manifestations of the Spirit is prophecy. Romans 12:6 says if our gift is prophesying then *"let us prophesy in proportion to our faith."* The gift of eternal life is the will of God for whosoever will believe and receive; the gift of the Holy Spirit and the gifts of the Spirit are the sovereign will of God for all His children. Nevertheless, it takes faith to appropriate any gift of God. For by grace, we are saved through faith.

Jesus continually told this truth to people who experienced the power of God: *"Your faith has made you whole;" "according to your faith be it unto you;"* and *"if you can believe, all things are possible to those who exercise their faith to believe"* (see Matt. 9:22; Mark 5:34; 10:52; Luke 8:48; 17:19; 18:42; Matt. 9:29; Eph. 1:19). We have the right and authority to turn the power switch on or off. To turn the faith switch on, one simply believes that Jesus meant what He said and said what He meant, and that God will do what He said He would do when we trust in and act upon His Word.

A blown fuse: When there is a short or an overload of electricity to a fuse, it melts or breaks the strip of wire that allows the transfer of electricity. This is called a blown fuse. Fear is a fuse blower. It short-circuits our faith. A small fuse that is blown can stop a great and powerful engine from operating. Fear is one of the greatest things that keep us from moving in the supernatural. First John 4:18 declares that there is no fear in love, but perfect love casts out fear. It says in Jude 1:20-21 that we keep ourselves in the love of God by praying in the Holy Spirit. Romans 5:5 declares that the love of God is shed abroad in our hearts by the Holy Spirit as we pray in our spirit language. So again, we see how praying in tongues plays a vital role in us continuing to have a victorious life and ministry. Praying with our spirit language saturates our spirit in the love of God. Then the faith which works by love can work mightily within us and through us, for the fullness of love casts out all fear. God's love and faith keep our fuses connected so that there can be a proper transfer and operation of the power of God in our lives.

Paul told Timothy, *"Stir up the gift of God which is in you...for God has not given us a spirit of fear, but of power and of love and of a sound mind"* (2 Tim. 1:6-7). We must not allow fear to blow our fuse and cut off the flow of divine power to our off and on switch, but continually allow the power to flow. With biblical understanding and a decisive act of our will, we can flip our switch of faith on and start operating in the power of God. The Holy Spirit transformer will determine the amount of power needed and the gift needed to accomplish the purpose of God. Remember that blown fuses can be replaced by live fuses. Unbelief can be replaced by faith; fear can be replaced by love. The truth of God's Word can remove the blown fuse of fear and praying in our spirit language can put the new workable fuse back in place.

70 REASONS CONTINUED...

TWENTY-SIX

Our spirit language is the major key that unlocks the door to our spirit life and all of the attributes of God and powerful manifestations of the Holy Spirit. The whole Christian life is lived and empowered by the Word of God and the Spirit of God. We receive the empowerment of the Word of God from reading and hearing preaching. The spirit language brings enlightenment on the Word and produces the fruit and manifestations of the Spirit (see Heb. 4:12; Rom. 10:14, 17; Acts 1:8; Gal. 5:22; 1 Cor. 12:7-11).

TWENTY-SEVEN

Our spirit language is the key to God's storehouse. Speaking in tongues is the car key that starts the engine, and continuing to pray in tongues works like the gas pedal that puts fuel into the engine and determines the power thrust and continuing speed of the car (see Matt. 16:19; Acts 1:8).

TWENTY-EIGHT

The Holy Spirit chose the tongue as the member of the body to receive His greatest gift. The Spirit knew that the tongue is the most powerful member of the body, for *"death and life are in the power of the tongue"* (Prov. 18:21). The tongue is the most influential and controlling member, for it is to the human body what the bridle bit is in the mouth of the horse. It is the small rudder that determines the direction of a ship. The tongue is a small flame of fire that can start a great forest fire. When we pray in tongues it sets aflame our new natures with heavenly passion. The tongue is the only thing that cannot be tamed by man. But God can tame it by immersing the tongue in the Holy Spirit, and then controlling the speaking of the tongue by a new spirit language that is not directed by the natural mind of man but by the redeemed spirit of man. The tongue speaking in its spirit language is the most powerful member in the spiritual Body of Christ. Speaking in tongues is like the heart beating and pumping life-giving blood into all the body (see James 3:2-8; Prov. 12:18; 15:4; 18:21; Matt. 12:37; John 6:63).

TWENTY-NINE

Speaking in tongues with our spirit language activates the spiritual hydroelectric power-producing plant that the Holy Spirit placed within us. It can be illustrated by different operations of a power plant, such as the great Hoover Dam. The reservoir filled with river water is the picture of a Christian being filled with the river of living waters of the Spirit. The water gate is our mouth that opens to let the water flow through. The turbine in the water gate is our tongue. The twirling of the blades of the turbine is the power that causes the rotation of the great dynamo in the heart of the dam. The dynamo is what generates the electrical power. Being filled with the Spirit, opening our mouth, and speaking in tongues begins a dynamo activity in our spirit that generates the power of God within us (see John 7:38; Acts 1:8; Eph. 3:20; Ps. 81:10).

THIRTY

Jesus said, *"Ye shall receive power, after that the Holy Ghost is come upon you"* (Acts 1:8 KJV). Notice that we receive the power AFTER the Holy Spirit comes and gives us that which produces the power. When the Holy Spirit comes to a person He gives him his own spirit language, which is what produces the power. The water in the reservoir of the dam is the same water on the other side of the dam, but it does not produce any power until it goes through the turbines. The reservoir of the Spirit within us does not produce any power until we open our mouth and begin speaking in tongues. The turbine of our power plant is speaking in tongues. A Spirit-baptized Christian has his own power plant that can produce the power he needs anytime he allows the water of life to flow through his mouth with speaking in tongues. Spirit-baptized

Christians should never lack for the power to perform since they have their own power-producing plants within them, which will produce power anytime they will pray in their spirit languages. *"I will pray with the spirit in tongues"* (1 Cor. 14:14).

THIRTY-ONE

Speaking in tongues may seem mechanical at times, but it is producing the presence and power of God in our lives like a dynamo. "A dynamo is an electric machine that converts energy from a mechanical form into an electrical form."[9] It is a natural operation, which can be seen and heard, that produces an invisible power called electricity. Speaking in tongues is a mechanical operation of speaking that can be seen and heard, but it is producing within us the invisible power and presence of God (see Acts 1:8; 1 Cor. 14:4).

THIRTY-TWO

A Christian not using his spirit language that the Holy Spirit deposited within him is like a person not writing checks on a million dollars someone deposited into his account. God's million dollar deposit of our spirit language is not a once-in-a-lifetime deposit. The Holy Spirit will continually keep the account filled if we will use the account for His Kingdom purposes (see Matt. 6:33).

THIRTY-THREE

Jude 1:20 declares that praying in tongues builds and increases faith in the believer. Faith is the procurer of all of God's promises. Faith is the medium of exchange for all heavenly things as money is the medium of exchange for all earthly things. A major way to increase our faith is to pray much more in the tongues of our spirit language. The gift of prophecy is typical of how we minister the gifts of the Spirit. "If a person's gift is prophecy, let him prophesy according to the proportion of his FAITH." Praying in tongues increases our proportion of faith (see Rom. 12:6; Jude 1:20; Mark 9:23; Matt. 9:29).

THIRTY-FOUR

An old, big Caterpillar™ motor had a little pony motor that was used to start the big powerful engine. Speaking in tongues is the Christian's pony motor that starts the engine of the manifestation of the powerful gifts of the Spirit (see 1 Cor. 12:8-10; 14:2).

ENDNOTES

1. Mario Pei, *The Living Webster Encyclopedic Dictionary of the English Language: With a Historical Sketch of the English Language* (Melrose Park, IL: Delair Publishing Company, Inc., 1981), 1064.

2. Ibid., 309.

3. Ibid.

4. W. E. Vine, *Vine's Expository Dictionary of New Testament Words* (McLean, VA: MacDonald Publishing, 1940), 737.

5. Ibid., 3.

6. Pei, *The Living Webster Encyclopedic Dictionary*, 1041.

7. Ibid., 396.

8. Ibid., 902.

9. Ibid., 309.

Chapter 6

Building Up and Downloading

Perceived Gain or Loss

There is a principle that people only desire and use what they feel is valuable to them. We eat, sleep, and exercise because our bodies need these things. We buy cars, computers, and cell phones because we see valuable uses for them, which create desire in us. In other words, we must see the value and purpose of something and how it will benefit us before we will pay the price to purchase it and then take the time to learn to use it properly.

The same is true with the gifts of God, whether it is the gift of eternal life, the gift of the Holy Spirit, or the gifts of the Holy Spirit. It is hard to convince sinners to receive the gift of eternal life unless you can make them see the value and need for them to accept Jesus to receive the gift. As we saw in the previous chapter, humankind is motivated to take action based on two things—the hope of gain or the fear of loss. People must see what they would gain by receiving and participating or what they would lose if they did not receive or participate. Paul wrote that he convinced people with the love of God, what they would gain, or else he motivated them with the terror of the Lord, what they would lose if they rejected the gospel (see 2 Cor. 5:11; Phil. 3:14; Matt. 13:45-46).

I seek to do the same in presenting the gift of the Holy Spirit. This book will emphasize all of the benefits and blessings in receiving and using our spirit language in all the varied ways and purposes. In case there are a few who may not be motivated by what they will gain by receiving and praying in their spirit languages, I quote the Scripture in Hebrews 2:3-4 where Paul tried to motivate the Hebrew Christians with the fear of loss, *"How shall we escape if we neglect so great a salvation...and gifts of the Holy Spirit."*

Jesus did the same in Matthew 25:14-30 when He revealed all that would be gained by using what we were given and then what would be lost if we did not use our talents or gifts. The person received great reward if the gift was faithfully used and increased, but the servant who did not use what was given was declared lazy and unprofitable and then cast into outer darkness where there will be weeping and gnashing of teeth. I prefer to be motivated by love for the truth and hope of gain than by the terror of the Lord and fear of loss. But the Bible says that Noah was moved with fear and built the ark (see Heb. 11:7). On the other hand, David was moved with love for God and destroyed the giant that was opposing Israel (see 1 Sam. 17:26, 45).

Regardless of what it takes to be motivated, receive and use your spirit language. Remember the spirit language was the greatest gift the Holy Spirit could give to the believer, just as Jesus was the greatest gift God could give for the redemption of the world. Let us now discover the many ways that we are to use this "greatest gift" that the Holy Spirit has given to us.

SPIRIT LANGUAGE—OUR SPIRIT-BATTERY CHARGER

"He who speaks in a tongue edifies himself, but he who prophesies edifies the church" (1 Cor. 14:4). Paul declared by revelation and from his vast experience in using his spirit language that when he

prayed in tongues it edified him personally. But, when he prophesied in his native language, and that of his audience, he edified the church.

Strong's Exhaustive Concordance[1] defines edifies as that which builds up, instructs, and improves morally or intellectually. Praying in our spirit language builds up our spirit man, improves our moral being, and enlightens our intellect. The term build up conveys several things: 1) a gradual accumulation, 2) to increase in size or intensity over time, 3) to charge a battery to build it back up to full power.

The word charge has several applications which also convey what praying in the Spirit does for an individual. When we pray in tongues it produces a gradual accumulation of the life and power of God within our spirit. As we continue to pray in our spirit language that power increases in size and intensity. To charge a battery is the process of storing energy chemically for conversion into electricity. Charging stores electrical energy into a battery so that it has the power to start the great engine of a vehicle. As we pray in our spirit language, the presence and power of God is stored in our spirit, which gives us the power to live the life of Christ and to manifest the power of God.

To charge a weapon is to fill it with the explosive to be detonated in order to fire a big gun. Jesus promised that we would receive power after we received the gift of the Holy Spirit. One meaning of that word power is "explosive," which means we receive the explosive we need to detonate the big gun of the gifts of the Spirit (see Acts 1:8).

REVELATION FROM A CAR BATTERY

I received a revelation of this truth in 1970 when I drove my Buick station wagon from our headquarters in San Antonio, Texas, to California. After taking care of my business, I got in my car to leave and discovered it wouldn't start because the battery was dead. My friend had a small car with a 6-volt battery. He said he could connect a jumper cable from his battery to mine and start the car. However, we discovered his 6-volt battery did not have enough power to charge my big 12-volt battery, which was designed to start my eight-cylinder, 430 horse power motor. That illustrated to me how some Christians do not have the power to activate someone else's spirit motor. They are 6-volt Christians trying to activate the motor of someone whose engine requires a 12-volt charge.

We then removed the battery from the car and took it to a shop with a battery charger. I knew nothing about mechanics or how cars operated at that time. I was very curious as to how they would charge my battery. The attendant took my battery over to a machine that had two cables extended from it and a screen in the box part. He clamped one of the cables onto a positive post and one on a negative post on top of the battery. He then turned a switch that directed an indicator, which stayed in the green portion instead of the red. I asked him why he did that. He said that it revealed whether my battery had a dead cell or not. If so, then he could charge it all day and it would not take the charge.

I immediately received a revelation as to why I could pray for some people for hours and they still did not receive the charge from the Lord. They each had a dead cell in their lives. Unbelief and sin causes dead cells in our battery, hindering us from receiving what we are desiring and others are praying for us to receive.

The mechanic then unscrewed the caps that covered several holes in the top of the battery. At my inquiry he explained that he was checking the water in the battery, for if it was low it would hinder the battery from being charged. I thought, 'Aha! We must keep filled with the Spirit, for if the river of life gets too low our spirit-batteries can lose their charge and not be able to start our spiritual engines.' The engine must start before the car can start moving and fulfilling its purpose.

After the attendant had filled all the cells with water, I asked him how I could tell if and when the battery was taking the charge. He said to watch the water—when it starts bubbling that is the proof that it is taking the charge of electricity that was flowing into it through the "laying on of hands" of the two clamps. The proof that a person is receiving and manifesting the gift of the Holy Spirit is when they start bubbling in other tongues. Jesus promised the river of life would bubble forth out of those who received the gift of the Holy Spirit (see John 7:37-39). I got excited when the water started bubbling because of the revelation and application it revealed.

He then asked me if I wanted a quick charge or a long charge. He said that if the generator on my car was working it would generate enough electrical power to fully charge my battery while I drove back to Texas. I believe our generator is the Holy Spirit working through our faith and obedience to flow life and power into the battery of our inner man. That's what Paul was saying when he wrote to the Ephesian Christians *"to be strengthened with might through His Spirit in the inner man"* (Eph. 3:16). And Jude wrote, *"Building yourselves up on your most holy faith, praying in the Holy Spirit"* (Jude 1:20).

Most of the time when I pray in tongues, I visualize my battery charger (spirit language) being plugged into the Holy Spirit outlet. That outlet is a line coming from the universal power plant— eternal, Almighty God. As I continue praying I know that my battery (spirit/inner man) is being charged with the life and power of God. I am being edified as the Holy Spirit instructs my spirit and improves my moral fiber and enlightens my intellect. One definition of build up is a period of preparation before an event. I pray much in my spirit language before any event of ministry or any situation where I will need supernatural wisdom and grace to be able to perform rightly. This is just a portion of the benefits that come from the greatest gift the Holy Spirit could possibly give to a child of God.

POWER-PRODUCING PRAYING

We need to understand an important point concerning our spirit language producing power. The car motor running in low idle will not charge the battery sufficiently. To give the full charge needed the car motor must be accelerated to a higher RPM. For the turbine to turn the big dynamo to produce electricity it must have a forceful flow of water. As we saw in the illustration of the Caterpillar™ bulldozer in the previous chapter, in order for the pony motor to start the big diesel engine it has to run fast and loud. Likewise, praying in tongues in a slow and low manner is good for meditation and producing God's peace and comforting presence. However, to produce the power of God and give the extra charge to our spirit, we must pray with more force, speed, and volume. This could be called "power-producing praying" where *the zeal of the Lord of Hosts will perform this"* (Isa. 9:7; 2 Kings 19:31).

This is especially true when we are preparing for spiritual warfare to pull down strongholds of the enemy and to cast out demons that are hindering God's purpose in our lives and ministries. It is forceful, fervent, and passionate praying that possesses the Kingdom of God. As the three illustrations portray, to give the maximum charge and empowerment to our inner spirit, we need to pray much louder and faster in our spirit language with the zeal of the Lord and the force of faith. Remember that the calm water in the reservoir does not produce any power. It takes water flowing forcefully through the water gate, spinning the turbine at a tremendous speed, and enabling it to rotate the great dynamo to produce the power (see Col. 3:23; James 5:16).

THE ACTIVATOR THAT STIRS UP

In Second Timothy 1:6 Paul admonished Timothy, *"I remind you to stir up the gift of God which is in you."* In other words, "Timothy, you stir up the gift of God which is within you. You stir up the gift." Paul did not explain how Timothy was to do that, so he must have previously been instructed in how to stir up one's gift. From Paul's teaching in First Corinthians 12–14 we discover what he must have taught and demonstrated to Timothy. He said that the Holy Spirit-given spirit language is the activator that stirs up the gifts and graces of God within the born-again, Spirit-baptized believer.

When Christians pray in their spirit languages from their spirit beings they stir up the divine gifts and attributes of the Christ within. This builds up their faith, which gives them boldness and power to act. Every gift is given by the grace of God, but received and activated by the faith of the believer. We have looked at the exhortation in Romans 12:6 that those who have the ministry or gift of prophecy should prophesy in proportion to their faith. By God's grace through our faith in Christ Jesus, the gift of eternal life is activated into our spirit being. The same is true for the Holy Spirit's gift and the gifts of the Holy Spirit. All the gifts of God are received and operated solely by grace and faith.

Praying in our spirit language pours more of God's grace into us and increases our faith, which enables us to personally manifest more of the life of Christ and minister more of the power of God to others. No wonder Paul emphatically declared, "I thank my God I speak in tongues!" In fact, the rest of that statement emphasizes that he was not only thankful for his spirit language but that he spoke in tongues much more than most Christians and other apostles (see 1 Cor. 14:18-22).

THE GREATEST REVELATION REGARDING THE SPIRIT LANGUAGE

The reason Paul prayed in his spirit language so much is because he had the greatest revelation of the many uses and purposes for praying in tongues. Almost 100 percent of what we know about speaking in tongues comes from the writings of Paul and his disciple and traveling companion, Dr. Luke, who wrote the book of Luke and Acts. This is also true concerning the gifts of the Holy Spirit, five-fold ministers, the revelation of the Church as the Body of Christ with individual members, the purpose and power of the resurrection of Christ, the second coming of Christ, the position and power of Christians seated in heavenly places in Christ Jesus, and several other areas that the other New Testament writers do not cover. We thank God for the writings of Apostle Paul.

God must have loved Paul's writings a great deal for He directed the Holy Spirit to choose fourteen of his writings to be books of the New Testament—more than all the rest of the writings of the apostles and prophets and other New Testament writers. The four Gospels are about the life, teaching, and ministry of Jesus Christ. They were written by Matthew, Mark, Luke, and John. Acts, the first of the epistles, was written by Luke. The following fourteen epistles, from Romans through Hebrews, were written by Paul (some theologians disagree about the authorship of Hebrews, but I believe the evidence points to Paul). James wrote one epistle, Peter two, John four, and Jude one. Since God put so much importance upon the writings of Apostle Paul, we should accept them as accurate, inspired by the Holy Spirit and a true revelation of the heart and mind of God. Paul is the greatest authority with the greatest revelation on the Holy Spirit's many valuable purposes for giving Christian believers their spirit languages.

DOWNLOADING MYSTERIES—THE DIVINE TRANSFER

God planned a special way to transfer His thoughts and power from His heart and mind to the hearts and minds of His children. In recent years we have developed a better understanding of this process through the function of computers. The word for this process in computer language is downloading. To download something is to copy data and transfer it from one computer to another, from a computer to a disk or from the Internet to a

computer. There is a Scripture that reveals that pray...
in our spirit language is like the act or process of downloa...

> *He who speaks in a tongue does not speak to men but to*
> *God, for no one understands him; however, in the spirit he*
> *speaks mysteries* (1 Corinthians 14:2).

SPIRIT HARD DRIVES

A computer's hard drive is its non-removable magnetic disk
with a large data-storage capacity. A master computer can transfer
to individual computers as much of its information as the smaller
computers are capable of receiving. When we pray in our spirit
language we connect with our master Spirit, God, who is like our
Master computer with an endless capacity of important information. When the Word says we speak mysteries it means that God
is downloading from his Spirit hard drive to our spirit hard drives.
His truth is stored in our spirit ready to be flashed on the screen of
our mind when needed.

We could also say our spirit language "uploads" our desires,
petitions, worship, and heart longings to God's hard drive. The
Bible speaks of our prayers ascending to God and being stored for
fulfillment in God's timing and purpose (see Rev. 5:8).

MYSTERIES DEFINED

The *Oxford English Dictionary*² defines mystery as: 1) something that is difficult or impossible to understand or explain; 2)
something hidden in secrecy or obscurity; 3) in Christian theology
a religious belief based on divine revelation. Strong's Concordance
states that the mysteries are secrets of God like the Old Testament
prophecies that were not understood until God revealed them to
the New Testament apostles. Mysteries are things not naturally or
readily understood. They require Holy Spirit revelation and application for the natural mind to understand.

...eal this truth:

> ...been hidden from ages and from
> ...een revealed to the saints. I am called
> ...riches of the glory of this mystery, which
> ...the hope of glory (Colossians 1:26-27).

> ...e known unto us the mystery of His will. By
> ...He made known to me the mystery of His will.
> When ...u read you may understand my knowledge in
> the mystery of Christ, which in other ages was not made
> known to the sons of men, but it has now been revealed
> by the Spirit to His holy apostles and prophets. To me was
> this grace given to make all see what is the fellowship of
> the mystery, which from the beginning has been hidden in
> God. This is a great mystery [husband and wife becoming
> one flesh], but I speak concerning Christ and His Church
> becoming one body of Christ. Pray for me that I may open
> my mouth and boldly proclaim the mystery of the gospel
> (Ephesians 1:9; 3:3-5, 9; 5:32; 6:19).

There are several other mysteries mentioned in the Bible, such
as the mystery of iniquity, mystery of the faith, mystery of God
and godliness, mystery of the seven stars, mystery of Babylon,
and the final mysteries of God that will be revealed by the prophets at the sounding of the seventh trumpet (see Col. 2:2; 4:3; 2
Thess. 2:7; 1 Tim. 3:9, 16; Rev. 1:20; 10:7; 17:5, 7; Rom. 16:24;
Mark 4:11).

REVELATION FROM FOUR HOURS OF SPEAKING IN TONGUES

In 1953, at the age of nineteen, I was attending Bible College
in Portland, Oregon. One day I drove down to Salem to minister
at a church. After the preaching ministry, all of us went to the

altar to pray. The Holy Spirit began to move in my praying in a way I had not experienced before. I could sense this was a sovereign move of God taking place and I should stay in place and let the Holy Spirit have His way in what He was doing until it was fully accomplished. I sat down crossed-legged so that I could be comfortable enough not to cause distraction. It ended up being a four-hour session that lasted till quite some time after midnight. I spent the entire four hours praying continuously in tongues. I had prayed in a variety of tongues after receiving the gift of the Holy Spirit. However, this was a new experience.

In my natural mind, it was like I was listening to two different people carry on a conversation. I had no terminology then to explain what was happening, but today I could say my spirit was uploading to God and God was downloading to my spiritual hard drive. Here is what was happening. My spirit would pray through my mouth for four or five minutes in a language that sounded like a romantic soft language, such as French, Spanish, or Italian. This language was expressed in a pleading, requesting, and beseeching tone. After a short period of time, my spirit language would change to a deeper, harder, more authoritative tone, like an African, German, or Russian language. I could feel the switch from my spirit talking to God then to God talking to my spirit. His was an instructive, commanding voice as one giving important directions and information. It felt like He was saying, "Watch out for this and be careful of that. This is going to happen and when it does, I will lead you. Fear not." The language was not understood by my natural mind, but my spirit conveyed to me the essence of what was being spoken. This continued for four solid hours.

About four months later, there was a great upheaval in the Bible College. Five of our teachers left the college. The students were in great confusion as to what to do. We wondered, "Is the president of the Bible College in the wrong? Or are the five teachers? What do the teachers know that we students don't know? Why has this happened?" I was fasting for days and praying for hours at a time seeking God to reveal what His will was for me.

He finally spoke to me telling me to not be afraid or overly concerned, for He already had it all worked out for me. He said, "You remember when you prayed those four hours and you and I communicated in the Spirit? During that time I put into your spirit what you were to do. I put in the wisdom and grace you would need in order to make the right decision and take the right action."

Today He probably would speak in modern technological terms. He would say: "I downloaded to your spirit-hard drive from My Holy Spirit-hard drive all the information and grace you will need. All you have to do now is to trust Me, push the button of revelation, and the information will flash on the screen of your mind. Push the button of faith and you will be directed by the right decisions and take the right actions. Everything needed has already been imparted and programmed into your spirit." Using computer language He would have said, "I preprogrammed your spirit to think and take the action that will progress you on to fulfill your destiny."

INVEST THE TIME

A computer will only function according to the programming of the master programmer. The more we pray in our spirit language the more time and opportunity we give God to download to us and program our spirit to direct our thinking and actions. When we pray in tongues mysteries are being revealed to our spirit man and secret hidden things are made known. Apostle John declared that the Holy Spirit would show us things to come, bring all things to our remembrance, enlighten and empower us to glorify Christ, manifest His life, and do the works that Christ did (see John 16:7-15; 14:12,16, 26).

If we want to be built up in God and edify our spirit with the charge of God's power, then we need to pray much in our spirit language. We need to use our spiritual battery charger often and make sure our generator is working. Praying in our spirit language causes us to be strengthened by His Spirit in our inner man. All works of God are accomplished by His Spirit and His Word. We can be filled with His Word by studying the Bible, memorizing Scripture, and listening to anointed biblical teaching and preaching. We are filled with His Spirit when we are baptized in the Holy Spirit. The baptism of the Holy Spirit gives us the gift of the Holy Spirit, which is the ability to pray in unknown tongues. Praying in our spirit language has many benefits. We have just covered two of the major benefits—the downloading of God's Spirit to our spirit and the building up of believers in the life of Christ and power of God.

70 REASONS CONTINUED...

THIRTY-FIVE

Praying in our spirit language charges and empowers our inner spirit beings like a battery charger charges a car battery. Charging a battery is the process of storing energy chemically for conversion into electricity. It stores electrical energy into a battery so that it has the power to start the great engine of a vehicle. Praying in our spirit languages stores the presence and power of God into our spirits, which gives us the power to live the life of Christ and to manifest the power of God (see 1 Cor. 14:4; Eph. 3:16).

THIRTY-SIX

The spirit language is the divine activator that stirs up and activates the grace and gifts of God in our lives. *"Stir up the gift of God which is in you"* (2 Tim. 1:6).

THIRTY-SEVEN

Praying in tongues downloads mysteries from the mind of Christ and imparts them into the hard drive of our spirits. Praying with our spirit language uploads to God our deepest longings, desires, worship, and praise (see 1 Cor. 14:2; John 16:1314).

ENDNOTES

1. James Strong, *Strong's Exhaustive Concordance of the Bible* (McLean, VA: MacDonald Publishing).

2. *The Oxford English Dictionary* (Oxford University Press, 1928, 1989).

CHAPTER 7

ACTIVATING THE FRUIT OF THE SPIRIT

CHRIST'S LIFE IN US

The authors of the epistles wrote mainly about believers fulfilling their calling of being the new man in Christ Jesus. They emphasized that a Christian is a born-again spirit being living in a mortal fleshly body. We are not to live from the fleshly desires and dictates of the carnal nature but to live in the Spirit and obey the desires and dictates of the divine nature we received from Christ (see 2 Pet. 1:4, Gal. 5:16-23). Several Scriptures speak of us being dead to sin and alive to God. I am crucified with Christ and now it is no longer I who live, but Christ who lives in me (see Gal. 2:20). Our life is hidden with Christ in God and Christ is our life (see Col. 3:3-4). When the Bible speaks of walking and living in the Spirit, it is talking about living the life of Christ. The more of His Spirit that is activated into our being, the more of the life of Christ we have and live.

My spirit language was given to me when my spirit was immersed/baptized in the Holy Spirit. Paul declared that when he prayed in tongues, *"My spirit prays but my understanding is unfruitful"* (1 Cor. 14:14). Though it is my spirit doing the talking in tongues, it is motivated, covered, enabled, and directed by the

Holy Spirit. It is a gift given to my redeemed human spirit, but it does not function separately from God's Spirit, for when I was joined to the Lord my born-again spirit became one with God's Spirit. First Corinthians 6:17-20 reveals:

> *But he who is joined to the Lord is one spirit with Him. Flee sexual immorality. Every sin that a man does is outside the body, but he who commits sexual immorality sins against his own body. Or do you not know that your body is the temple of the Holy Spirit who is in you, whom you have from God, and you are not your own? For you were bought at a price; therefore glorify God in your body and in your spirit, which are God's.*

Our body and spirit become Christ's spirit-body, in which Christ lives His life and manifests His works on earth.

ACTIVATING THE FRUIT OF THE SPIRIT

The word activate means to make active or operative. It takes something from an inactive state and causes it to become functional. The majority of Christians allow the gift of the Holy Spirit and the gifts of the Holy Spirit that are within them to be inactive. They either desire to manifest the gifts but do not know how or they are like the servant who received one talent but was afraid to use it.

In the early 1980s I started teaching people how to use their gift of the Holy Spirit and gifts of the Spirit. Second Timothy 1:6 was one of the main Scriptures I used to challenge the saints. As we have seen, in this Scripture Paul challenged Timothy with the charge for him to "stir up the gift of God which is in you." Rather than quote this Scripture every time to emphasize this truth, I chose the one word that exemplified the truth: "activate." The word activate fully describes and expresses the same meaning as "stir up."

We have developed more than fifty "activations" that activate the different manifestations of the Spirit that are within the saints. An activation is a faith action that a believer acts upon in order to activate a manifestation of the Spirit. The history of the New Testament Church is called the Book of Acts. It records all the acts the apostles did to establish the Church, live the life of Jesus, and do the works of Christ.

THE FIRST ACTIVATION—THE SINNER'S PRAYER

Having sinners repeat and pray the "sinner's prayer" is the first activation established in the Church. Evangelical ministers are the ones who developed this activation. They would preach a salvation message to their audience and then give an invitation for sinners to come forward. The preacher would have them repeat what they called the "sinner's prayer." The minister would say the words of repentance one phrase at a time and the sinners would repeat what was said. They were instructed to believe in their hearts what they were confessing with their mouths. By all these actions—coming forward, standing, praying, and confessing their sins and accepting Jesus as their Savior—the minister would then assure them that they had been born again and their names were written in the Lamb's book of life.

The sinner's prayer activation imparts the gift of eternal life into a person's spirit. It has proven to be a workable activation, because multimillions over hundreds of years have become children of God by praying the sinner's prayer. Evangelicals developed this activation to receive the gift of eternal life.

THE SECOND ACTIVATION

Pentecostals and Charismatics developed the activation for born-again Christians to receive the gift of the Holy Spirit with the evidence of speaking in tongues. The minister or leader would first teach on the scriptural reality of speaking in tongues. He would then have the seekers ask the Lord to give them the gift of the Holy Spirit with speaking in tongues. Then the minister would lay hands on them, praying and declaring for them to receive the gift of the Holy Spirit. If a seeker did not begin to speak immediately in tongues, then he or she was encouraged and instructed how to exercise his faith to receive the gift (see Luke 11:12-13).

ACTIVATION FOR THE GIFTS OF THE HOLY SPIRIT

The Prophetic-Apostolic Movement ministers developed the activation for activating Spirit-baptized saints in the gifts of the Holy Spirit. The Lord gave me a revelation and sovereign experience in the 1970s that enabled me to develop the activation for saints ministering the manifestations of the Holy Spirit. We called it an "activation" for prophetic ministry because we majored in the ministry of prophesying. The activation consists of teaching, activating, and training saints to share with another person some thoughts from the heart of God and mind of Christ. It is called "one-to-one sharing" and is based on First Peter 4:10, *"As each one has received a gift, minister it one to another...."* This activation has proven to be as true and workable in activating saints in the gifts of the Spirit as the "sinner's prayer" has been in activating the gift of eternal life.

TESTED, TRIED, AND PROVEN TRUE

I trained others to use this activation and now our 3,000 Christian International ministers and equipped saints have activated more than 250,000 believers into prophetic ministry. When I speak of prophetic-apostolic ministry I am speaking of all the manifestations of the Holy Spirit. This prophetic ministry is for all saints, just as the gift of eternal life is for all sinners and the gift of the Holy Spirit is for all Christians who will believe and receive. Apostle Paul declared, *"The manifestation of the Spirit is given to each one* [believer] *for the profit of all."* He also stated, *"You can all prophesy"* and, *"As each one has received a gift, minister it to one another, as good stewards of the manifold grace of God"* (1 Cor. 12:7; 14:31; 1 Pet. 4:10).

ACTIVATIONS EXERCISE
SPIRITUAL SENSES

To be activated means that you are doing a spiritual exercise which activates your spiritual senses. Hebrews 5:12-14 speaks of Christians who have become dull of hearing and are not growing and maturing in Christ's life and ministry. They have remained baby Christians who can only partake of milk and not solid food. For solid food belongs to those who are of full age, that is, those "who by reason of use have their senses exercised to discern both good and evil."

I teach at our training sessions that we practice "ESS" and "ESG," but not "ESP." We practice activating our faith, Exercising our Spiritual Senses (ESS), and Exercising Spiritual Gifts (ESG), but we do not promote the psychic practice of Extra Sensory Perception (ESP). To discern good is to discern and determine the thoughts of God, the gifts of the Spirit, and what is a manifestation of the Holy Spirit. To discern evil is to discern a demonic suggestion, including demonic influence on the imagination of man or the natural man's spirit and ideas. Natural man trying to manifest spiritual things from his psychic and soulish realms is what some call "being in the flesh" and not "in the Spirit."

SPIRITUAL DISCERNMENT VS. THE GIFT
OF DISCERNING OF SPIRITS

Not only must we learn to discern between good and evil, but we must learn to discern what is naturally good but not necessarily

God. It requires a spiritual and mature person to be able to discern the difference between a good idea and a God idea. Spiritual discernment is not the same as the gift of the discerning of spirits. Spiritual discernment is an ability acquired through the experience of exercising our spiritual senses in activations until we are mature and skilled in discerning whether something is of God or not of God.

For example, Zerubbabel was wondering how he would finish the building of the temple and all the work that God wanted him to do. The word of the Lord came to him with this declaration, *"'Not by might, nor by power, but by My Spirit,' says the Lord of Hosts"* (Zech. 4:6). The might and power of man's own wisdom and strength cannot do the work of God. It requires the enablement and work of the Holy Spirit to accomplish the work of the Lord. One reason this book is being written is to help believers receive more of the Spirit of God so they can be more like Jesus and accomplish the greater works of Christ. We must discover the activator to spiritual power in order to increase our spirituality and discernment in knowing the mind of Christ and manifesting the supernatural power of God (see 1 Cor. 2:10-16).

THE GREAT ACTIVATOR

As we mentioned in Chapter 1, Jesus was the greatest gift God could find to give to humankind. The Holy Spirit was the greatest gift Jesus could give to the Church. The Holy Spirit searched all that God is and has to find the best and greatest gift He could give a child of God living on earth. He evaluated all of God's wisdom, power, attributes, and resources. They were all great, but could He give each one everything? At last He discovered the greatest gift He could give. It was the gift that could activate any and all of the attributes of God. He would give to the individual saint that which could activate and appropriate all the blessings of God. It would be the great activator.

On that great Pentecostal feast day the Holy Spirit birthed the Church that Jesus had purchased with His own life's blood. The Holy Spirit then gave each member of the Church His own personal gift for them. He baptized their spirits with the ability to pray in an intelligent communicating language. They would pray in languages of angels and men—languages never learned with their natural minds. Their spirit languages would bypass their natural minds and go directly to God. This gift would provide spirit-to-Spirit communication. It was the greatest and most beneficial gift that the Holy Spirit could possibly give to the individual child of God. Believers now had another Helper that would help them relate to God and appropriate all that Jesus provided for His Church. The Holy Spirit's gift of the believer's spirit language is the great activator to appropriate all that the believer is to be and do.

FOUR INGREDIENTS IN THE FORMULA FOR ACTIVATING

Every formula that produces a desired result has to have the right ingredients in the proper amounts. To produce water you must have the ingredients of two parts hydrogen and one part oxygen, or H2O. All chemists know the reality of this—and so do homemakers who bake cakes.

Like ingredients in a formula, there are four principles involved in an activation that must be practiced for it to be workable. The first three are the preparation and foundation for the fourth, while the fourth is the actual act or activation. I have used these four principles to activate thousands in prophetic ministry and the gifts of the Holy Spirit. These are the same four principles that are involved in the activation called the sinner's prayer. The same four principles are involved in receiving and manifesting spiritual gifts and the fruit of the Holy Spirit.

THE FOUR ACTIVATION PRINCIPLES

1. Hear and Understand the Biblical Truth on the Matter

ROMANS 10:17

"Faith comes by hearing, and hearing by the word of God." Word here refers to a rhema—a Spirit-quickened word.

JOHN 8:32

"And you shall know the truth, and the truth shall make you free." The truth of what is available to us makes us free to believe for it.

EPHESIANS 3:3

"...by revelation He made known to me the mystery..."

JUDE 1:20

"...building yourselves up on your most holy faith, praying in the Holy Spirit." Spirit language praying brings revelation and builds up faith.

2. Believe in the Heart

ROMANS 10:8-10

Faith is located in the heart and with the heart man believes. Head-intellect cannot believe; it can only gather faith-building material.

MATTHEW 12:34

"...out of the abundance of the heart the mouth speaks."

JOHN 6:28

What must we do to work the works of Christ? Believe!

MARK 9:23

"If you can believe, all things are possible to him who believes."

JOHN 5:4

Believing faith is the victory and the medium of exchange for all heavenly things, just as money is the medium of exchange for all earthly things.

FIRST CORINTHIANS 14:4; JUDE 1:20

Spirit language praying builds up one's spirit and increases faith within the believer, taking him or her from faith to greater faith.

3. Speak With the Mouth

GENESIS 1–2

God created all of earth's creation by His spoken word.

ROMANS 10:8-10

Faith is in the mouth and mouth confession produces salvation. Words spoken with heart-faith activate that which is spoken into manifestation.

PSALM 116:10

"I believed, therefore I spoke." Words from the mouth reveal the amount of faith in the heart. Words are faith's measuring stick.

PROVERBS 18:21

"Death and life are in the power of the tongue." The words we speak activate faith or deaden it, resulting in spirit manifestations or works of the flesh.

4. Take Action

One's whole being unified in faith-action activates and obtains. James 2:14-26: Eight times "faith" is declared dead (non-faith) without action.

V. 14

Faith without works does not profit.

V. 17

Faith by itself without works is dead.

V. 18

I demonstrate my faith by my works.

V. 20

"Do you want to know, O foolish man, that faith without works is dead?"

V. 21

The faith of Abraham was working together with his works/action and by works his faith was made perfect (no biblical faith without action).

V. 24

A man is justified by works/action and not by faith only.

V. 26

"For as the body without the spirit is dead, so faith without works is dead also."

The first principle of an activation is having a proper biblical education on the scriptural fact that the gift is for every believer and it can be received by faith. A conscientious and sincere Christian will not and cannot believe for something unless they are convinced that it is according to God's Word and will. The main subject of this book is biblical understanding on the gift of the Holy Spirit. When a person does not have a thorough comprehension of the power and purpose of praying in his spirit language then he rarely prays in tongues. And when he does pray in tongues it is not done in faith with understanding of what is being accomplished.

Therefore, there is first the need of biblical understanding concerning the matter of speaking in unknown tongues. When the biblical truth is understood it sets the Christian free from doubt and fear concerning the gift. It gives him assurance and security to receive the Holy Spirit's gift of the spirit language.

The second principle for receiving the gift of the Holy Spirit or manifesting the supernatural works of Christ Jesus is to believe with the heart. The natural mind is not designed to believe. Its job is to gather all the scriptural proof, teaching, preaching, and testimonials on the subject and send the information to the heart in a convincing manner. The Bible does not say that hearing the word is faith, but it does say "faith comes" by hearing and receiving a *rhema*-word. Faith is like a seed; it is planted in the heart and nourished until it sprouts. Then it is cultivated until it is matured for harvest, when it is able to procure whatever has been requested. Faith comes to the place where it is strong and positive enough to do its job.

There are three levels of faith: 1) Saving faith or initial faith for salvation. 2) The fruit of faith, of which everyone is given a measure or seed that can be grown to the place it produces edible fruit. 3) The gift of faith, which is one of the supernatural manifestations of the Spirit. The fruit of faith is all that is necessary for most activations.

The third principle is speaking with our mouth. The believer must know that the gift is for him and then believe in his heart for it, but he will still not possess it without the next activation principle of speaking with the mouth. With the heart man believes unto righteousness (see Rom. 10:10). Believing in the heart puts the person in the right relationship with God, the right position, the right attitude, and the right thinking. But believing with the heart without speaking with the mouth does not possess or produce. With the mouth, confession is made unto saving, delivering, producing, possessing, and becoming that for which the heart believes.

If you want to know how much faith you have for what you have requested in prayer, listen to your mouth when you speak about the matter. Faith speaks and calls those things that are not as though they already are. Faith is a present tense word. NOW faith is! Faith is now! Faith is the substance or the assurance of the thing hoped for and faith is the evidence of that which cannot be seen (see Heb. 11:1). Hope believes for the future, but faith believes for the present. Faith is motivated by the Spirit and acts only on the Word of God. The more of the Spirit and Word we activate into our lives, the more of Christ's presence and power we will have and demonstrate. Praying in our spirit language plays a vital role in producing the power and presence of God in our lives.

The fourth principle is taking action. You can know the truth, believe it in your heart and talk about it with your mouth, but if you do not take action nothing happens like it is supposed to. According to Apostle James, there is no true faith without corresponding action. Faith is not just a mental attitude, but an action taken. All actions may not be faith motivated, but it is certain that one cannot have living biblical faith without action. For faith without works is profitless and nonproductive (see James 2:14-26). In fact, professed faith that does not take action is as dead as a human body without a living spirit within it. There are live human bodies and there are dead human bodies. There is dead inactive faith and there is living active faith. So how do we activate our faith into being alive, profitable, and productive?

UNDERSTANDING BIBLICAL TERMINOLOGY

Praying with the spirit or praying in the Holy Spirit is saying the same thing as praying in tongues or with your spirit language. Praying in tongues is a spirit operation; it activates your spirit into active service. The fruit of the Spirit mentioned in Galatians 5:22-23 originate from the Spirit, are attributes of the Spirit, and are a Spirit operation. They are just as supernatural as the nine gifts of the Spirit as both are given and manifested by the Spirit. The nine gifts or manifestations of the Spirit listed in First Corinthians 12:8-10 originate in the Holy Spirit, are manifestations of the Spirit, and are gifts given to the saints by the Holy Spirit.

THE SPIRIT LANGUAGE BUILDS UP ONE'S FAITH

Jude wrote a letter to Christians exhorting them to build themselves up in their most holy faith by praying in their spirit languages. *"But you, beloved, building yourselves up on your most holy faith, praying in the Holy Spirit, keep yourselves in the love of God"* (Jude 1:20). The love of God is poured into our hearts by the Holy Spirit who has been given to us (see Rom. 5:5). These Scriptures reveal that love and faith are activated by the spirit language that the Holy Spirit has given us. Love and faith are two of the nine fruits of the Holy Spirit, which the Scriptures say are imparted and activated by praying in tongues. Therefore, all nine of the fruits of the Holy Spirit are shown to be activated and increased within us by praying in our spirit language.

NINE PERSONAL BENEFITS OF PRAYING IN TONGUES

Galatians 5:22-23 lists nine attributes of God calling them the fruit of the Spirit: *"The fruit of the Spirit is love, joy, peace, longsuffering, kindness, goodness, faith, gentleness and self-control."* As previously mentioned, when we pray with the Holy Spirit in our spirit language it generates and activates the attributes of God called the fruit of the Spirit. This is all important because God's highest calling and predestined purpose is for every Christian to be conformed to the image of His son Jesus Christ. *"For whom*

God foreknew, He also predestined, to be conformed to the image of His Son" (Rom. 8:29). God the Father's predestined purpose was for Jesus to become the prototype and the firstborn of many who would become just like Him. Hebrews 2:10 declares, *"It was fitting for Jesus, for whom are all things and by whom are all things, in bringing many sons to glory."* Jesus was the glory of God which means He was the express image and likeness of God. For Jesus to bring many sons unto His glory means that He is bringing them to His likeness and image.

That is the reason the Bible exhorts Christians to grow in the grace and knowledge of Jesus Christ and to continue to go from glory to glory by the Spirit of the Lord until they are transformed into Christ's image (see 2 Cor. 3:18). The names given to the fruit of the Spirit are descriptive words of the nature and character of Christ Jesus. The more of the fruit of the Spirit that becomes incorporated into our lives, the more we become conformed into the nature, character, and image of Christ. Our spirit language has the power and ministry from the Holy Spirit to generate, activate, and increase the fruit of the Spirit into our nature and character. This is one of the major reasons the Holy Spirit chose the spirit language of praying in unknown tongues as the greatest gift He could find in all of Heaven and earth to give to those Jesus redeemed by His life's blood. It was the one gift that could produce and activate all the other gifts and attributes of God.

Let us now discover the benefits we obtain by increasing the fruit of the Spirit in our lives as we pray more and more in our spirit language.

THE FRUIT OF LOVE

The Holy Spirit's fruit of love is more than a fruit. For the Scripture declares that God is Love (see 1 John 4:8, 16). So the more of God's love we receive, the more godly we will be. Fear is one of the greatest hindrances to Christians living the life of

Christ and manifesting the supernatural. The solution is more love, because there is no fear in love, but perfect love casts out fear. If a person is still fearful, then they have not been made perfect in love (see 1 John 4:2–5:3). If we really know the love of Christ in its width and length, depth and height, it will enable us to be filled with the fullness of God and continually be strengthened with might by His Spirit in the inner man (see Eph. 3:16-19).

The thirteenth chapter of First Corinthians makes God's love more valuable, needed, and important to have than anything else. In fact, every action and ministry that is not motivated by love counts for nothing in God's sight. The only thing that counts is faith which works by love (see Gal. 5:6). The Word of God declares that we can be Charismatics speaking with the tongues of men and angels, but if we do not have love, we become no more than noise, like sounding brass or clanging cymbals. It reveals we can be Prophetic-Apostolic saints with the gift of prophecy and can understand all mysteries, but if we have not love we are nothing. We can be "Faith People" with faith to move mountains, but if we have not the love of God working in us, we count for nothing in God's sight. It declares we can be modernistic Protestants or Catholics with a great humanitarian concern to the extent that we bestow all our goods to feed the poor or even allow our bodies to be burned, but if we have not love all this effort profits us nothing (see 1 Cor. 13:13).

This agape love that is so necessary is not just an emotional compassionate feeling but consists of the very attributes of God and the character of Christ. Paul does not leave us wondering what love is; he uses several words to describe what God's love really is:

> *Love suffers long and is kind; love does not envy; love does not parade itself, is not puffed up; does not behave rudely, does not seek its own, is not provoked, thinks no evil; does not rejoice in iniquity, but rejoices in the truth; bears all*

things, believes all things, hopes all things, endures all things.

Love never fails. But whether there are prophecies, they will fail; whether there are tongues, they will cease; whether there is knowledge, it will vanish away.

And now abide faith, hope, love, these three; but the greatest of these is love (1 Corinthians 13:4-8, 13).

Love alone includes most of the attributes in the fruit of the Spirit. That is one reason love is declared to be the greatest.

Apostle John recorded Jesus' words that we demonstrate that we love God and have His love in us when we keep the commandments of God and love the brethren (see John 15:9-10). The feeling of love is good, but the works of love are greater. If we love God, we will keep His commandments. One of the commandments of Jesus to His disciples was, *"He commanded them not to depart from Jerusalem, but to wait for the promise of the Father"* (Acts 1:4). Jesus knew that the promise of the Father was the gift of the Holy Spirit, and when the disciples received the gift of their spirit language they would have the ability to keep themselves in the love of God. They could increase the receiving and demonstrating of God's love by praying in the Holy Spirit's gift since He is the One who appropriates and distributes God's love and the gifts of the Spirit.

Paul declared that the love of God is poured into our heart and increased by the Holy Spirit and His gift (tongues) which He has given to us. We can be filled with more of God's love as we pray more in our spirit language. If you really want to grow in love, then invest more time praying in tongues (see Rom. 5:5).

THE FRUIT OF JOY

The Kingdom of God is righteousness, peace, and joy in the Holy Spirit (see Rom. 14:7). Jesus said to His disciples, *"These things I have spoken to you, that My joy may remain in you, and that your joy may be full"* (John 15:11). Joy is about more than making us feel good, *"for the joy of the Lord is your strength"* (Neh. 8:10). Joy enables us to fulfill the scriptural command to *"be strong in the Lord and in the power of His might"* (Eph. 6:10). We are to *"rejoice always...in everything give thanks"* (1 Thess. 5:16, 18). The place of joy is in His presence, where we are filled with Christ's presence, as we pray in our spirit language. There is nothing more important than to be filled with the presence of God. God inhabits the praises of His people with His presence (see Ps. 22:3). Apostle Paul said, *"I will sing with the spirit, and I will also sing with the understanding"* (1 Cor. 14:15). Worshiping and singing praises to God in tongues causes our inner being to be filled with the presence of God.

SPEAKING OF THE WONDERFUL WORKS OF GOD BRINGS JOY

The 120 who spoke in other tongues on the Day of Pentecost were all local people who spoke Hebrew, and some of them may have known another language such as Greek. Acts 2:5 says there were Jews gathered in Jerusalem from every nation. But the ones who were speaking in tongues were all Galileans. It lists about fourteen of the different dialects and languages represented. The Jews from the nations were amazed and marveled that they were hearing these Galileans speaking in their language. They said, *"We hear them speaking in our own tongues the wonderful works of God"* (Acts 2:11). The point in rehearsing the original outpouring of the disciples speaking in other tongues is for us to take notice that they were speaking "the wonderful works of God."

Paul revealed that when we pray in tongues it could be in a heavenly tongue of angels or a language of some tribe or nation on earth. I have heard many testimonies of people understanding the "other tongues" that a person was speaking, meaning that they were speaking in an actual human language that they had never studied. In every instance, the person who could understand the language said the one speaking was expressing much praise to God and talking of His wonderful works.

When we pray in tongues we are speaking praises to God which God inhabits with His presence. In His presence is fullness of joy. We can increase the amount of the fruit of joy in our lives by praying in our spirit language.

THE FRUIT OF PEACE

The peace of God is so essential in so many areas of our lives. The peace of God keeps our hearts and minds and surpasses all understanding (see Phil. 4:6). It is a characteristic of the spiritual mind. *"To be spiritually minded is life and peace"* (Rom. 8:6). Peace is an indicator of the leading of the Lord. *"For you shall go out with joy, and be led out with peace"* (Isa. 55:12). Jesus is the Prince of Peace and the King of Peace (see Isa. 9:6; Heb. 7:2). Jesus told His disciples, *"Peace I leave with you, My peace I give to you"* (John 14:27). *"And the God of peace will crush Satan under your feet shortly"* (Rom. 16:20). Perfect peace has those whose mind is stayed on the Lord (see Isa. 26:3). The Kingdom of God is peace in the Holy Spirit (see Rom. 14:17). Praying in one's spirit language activates the fruit of peace in our heart and illuminates our minds with the peace that surpasses all understanding. You can sense the peace of God flooding your soul as you pray for some time in your spirit language.

In my position as Bishop over thousands of ministers and five major organizations, plus my family and personal life, I am continually bombarded with reports that could take away my peace. When you first hear a bad report, it immediately gives a heart-sickening feeling, anxiety, worry, and definitely not a sense of peace. In order to counteract the bad report, I begin immediately to pray in my spirit language until His peace is activated and supersedes the feelings brought by the bad report. My heart and mind are then cleared to remember the positive promises of God, and my inner being is filled with the presence of God.

The outward life is continually challenging our inner lives with the negative things of this world. The major way we can defend ourselves against these attacks and overcome the devilish world is to be reinforced on the inside and build a force field around us with the shield of faith. The shield of faith could be illustrated by the fictional Star Trek Enterprise ship, which has an inner generator that can generate a force field around the ship. Spirit-baptized Christians have an inner generator that can produce a force field around us with the shield of faith. As we continue to pray in tongues it generates the peace of God within and enables us to fulfill the scriptural command to *"Let the peace of God rule in your hearts"* (Col. 3:15).

THE FRUIT OF FAITH

The fruit of faith and love are the two key fruits. Love is the motivator and faith is the appropriator. Love motivates but faith appropriates. Galatians 5:6 says the only thing that counts with God is faith motivated by love. The Bible magnifies faith and love as the two most needed attributes of God. The fruit of faith is the same faith that is one of the pieces of the Christian's armor. In the description of the armor, the Scripture says, *"above all, taking the shield of faith with which you will be able to quench all the fiery darts of the wicked one"* (Eph. 6:16). Apostle John, who is known as the apostle of love, mentioned love more than one hundred times in his writings. Though his emphasis was love, he declared that faith is the victory that overcomes (see 1 John 5:4). The Scriptures reveal that without love we are nothing, and without faith we can do nothing (see 1 Cor. 13:1-3; Heb. 11:6). These two enable us to be and do—to be like Christ and do His wonderful works.

Faith is the currency of Heaven, but love is the printing press that produces the currency. Counterfeit money is that which is not printed by the government of the nation. Faith that is not motivated by the love of God is a counterfeit faith. We must make sure our faith is motivated and working by love.

Nevertheless, faith works regardless of its motivation. Jesus continually said, *"According to your faith let it be to you"* and, *"If you can believe, all things are possible to him who believes"* (Matt. 9:29; Mark 9:23). Jesus never gave any qualifications in order for faith to receive from God and manifest His power. Paul said that we are to minister in prophecy according to the proportion of our faith (see Rom. 12:6). It was God's love that gave the gifts to the Holy Spirit to distribute to the saints. Though they were given by the love of God, they are ministered by the faith of the believer.

THE FAITH INCREASER

Jesus' disciples asked Him to increase their faith. Instead of touching them and imparting more faith, He revealed to them that He was going to send another Helper—the gift of the Holy Spirit. Jesus knew that the Holy Spirit's gift of a spirit language would have the ability and ministry of building faith within His followers. It would work like a battery charger charging a battery, a pony motor on a big Caterpillar™, and a power-producing plant within them. If we really want to see our faith increase, then we must use the means by which the Holy Spirit gave—praying in tongues with our spirit language.

The two greatest ways to increase faith are with the Word of God and the Spirit of God. We can fill our heart and mind with the Word and empower our spirit by praying in tongues. The Word is the wood but the spirit language is what sets it on fire. We can grow the fruit of faith by continually hearing the Word of God and praying more often and for longer periods of time in our spirit language.

THE FRUIT OF LONGSUFFERING, KINDNESS, GOODNESS, GENTLENESS, AND TEMPERANCE

Those who have these fruits within their lives would have the same traits as those who truly are "ladies" and "gentlemen."

They are good, kind, gentle, full of patience, and full of self-control. Many pages could be written on the virtues of these remaining fruits of the Spirit. However the purpose of this book is not to give a long treatise on each, but to show that they can be activated and increased in our lives by praying in our spirit language. The fruit of the Spirit comes into a person when they are born of the Spirit. They are planted in our lives as nine different seeds that are to be watered and cultivated until they grow to maturity. They are to infiltrate our nature and personality until they become our new nature and way of life.

The Apostle Peter declared:

...by which have been given to us exceedingly great and precious promises, that through these you may be partakers of the divine nature, having escaped the corruption that is in the world through lust.

But also for this very reason, giving all diligence, add to your faith virtue, to virtue knowledge, to knowledge self-control, to self-control perseverance, to perseverance godliness, to godliness brotherly kindness, and to brotherly kindness love. For if these things are yours and abound, you will be neither barren nor unfruitful in the knowledge of our Lord Jesus Christ. For he who lacks these things is shortsighted, even to blindness, and has forgotten that he was cleansed from his old sins.

Therefore, brethren, be even more diligent to make your call and election sure, for if you do these things you will never stumble; for so an entrance will be supplied to you abundantly into the everlasting kingdom of our Lord and Savior Jesus Christ (2 Peter 1:4-11).

This exhortation of Apostle Peter on the need of adding and growing the attributes of God should convince us to grow in the fruit of the Spirit in every way that we possibly can. He said that if we have these in operation we will never stumble. But if we do not have the fruit and add to it then we are shortsighted and on the verge of being blinded. However, if we act upon his exhortation, he gives us the assurance that an eternal entrance into Christ's everlasting Kingdom would be abundantly supplied to us.

Thank Father God for giving us His Son for our redemption. Let us be appreciative to Jesus for giving the Holy Spirit to His Church for birthing, enlightening, empowering, and maturing. We can really be personally thankful that the Holy Spirit chose the greatest gift for us to have as individual Christians. The gift of our spirit language germinates and grows the fruit of the Spirit, which keeps us from stumbling and maintains 20/20 vision in our calling and life in Christ. If there were not all the other numerous benefits for praying in tongues, the ones mentioned in this chapter should be more than enough to motivate us to pray as much as we possibly can in our spirit language.

70 REASONS CONTINUED...

THIRTY-EIGHT

Our spirit prayer language germinates the seed of our spiritual fruit tree for sprouting and growing to a productive stage. The fruit of the Spirit is imparted into our spirits in seed form. Praying in the spirit language produces the nourishment for growing the fruit of the Spirit in a Christian's life. In fact, anything that is a spirit from God can be activated, such as the seven spirits of God, the spirit of wisdom and revelation, spirit of truth, spirit of life, etc.

It takes Spirit to activate spiritual things. Speaking in tongues was given to be a spirit activator (see Eph. 1:17; Rom. 1:4; 8:2).

THIRTY-NINE

The spirit language is a formula and activation for producing spiritual things just like the four principles of activation are a formula for activating any gift of God. The first principle is to know the biblical truth about the subject. The next three principles are to believe in your heart, confess with your mouth, and take action. The same is true for receiving and ministering the benefits of our spirit languages (see Rom. 10:8-10; John 8:32).

FORTY

Praying in tongues activates the fruit of the Spirit - love, joy, peace, longsuffering, kindness, goodness, faith, gentleness, and self control. Activating each of these nine fruits by praying in tongues gives us nine major reasons for praying much in our spirit languages. There is great importance and valuable benefits to having each of these spiritual attributes become active and mature in us. Just the first one alone—love—has most of the attributes and characteristics of Christ. Therefore, praying in tongues helps us to fulfill God's predestined purpose for us to be conformed to the image of His Son (see Gal. 5:22-23; 2 Cor. 3:18; 1 Cor. 13:1-13; Rom. 8:29).

CHAPTER 8

ACTIVATING THE GIFTS OF THE SPIRIT

HOLY SPIRIT GIFTS VS. THE GIFT OF THE HOLY SPIRIT

The gift of eternal life and the gift of the Holy Spirit are given mainly for the benefit of the individual. The Holy Spirit's gift of the spirit language is given to a born-again believer for their own self edification. Speaking in tongues was not given to bless others but to bless one's own spirit and soul. This book is covering all the numerous and diverse ways praying in our spirit language blesses us. In the last chapter on the fruit of the Spirit we showed how the spirit language activates and increases the nine attributes of God that the Scriptures call the fruit of the Spirit. They are expressions of the nature and character of Christ Jesus. Activating and growing the fruit attributes of God helps us to be transformed into Christ's image and likeness, thereby fulfilling His predestined purpose for each of His children. In this chapter we will show how praying in tongues with our spirit language can stimulate and activate the gifts of the Spirit.

THE GIFTS OF THE HOLY SPIRIT

The gifts of the Spirit are given to believers to meet the needs of humankind. They are the nine manifestations of the Spirit. They are described in First Corinthians 12:8-10:

For to one is given the word of wisdom through the Spirit, to another the word of knowledge through the same Spirit, to another faith by the same Spirit, to another gifts of healings by the same Spirit, to another the working of miracles, to another prophecy, to another discerning of spirits, to another different kinds of tongues, to another the interpretation of tongues.

The gifts demonstrate that our God and Savior Jesus Christ is alive and active in the world today. The vocal gifts show that God speaks to and through His people. The revelation gifts reveal that our God is omniscient, knowing all things about everything and everyone, and He reveals some of those things to His people. The power gifts reveal that our God is omnipotent and demonstrates His power over demons, humankind, and nature.

THE NINE MANIFESTATIONS OR GIFTS OF THE HOLY SPIRIT

» Vocal Gifts: Tongues, Interpretation of Tongues, Prophecy

» Revelation Gifts: Word of Knowledge, Word of Wisdom, Discerning of Spirits

» Power Gifts: Gift of Faith, Gifts of Healings, Working of Miracles

The nine gifts can be divided into three different categories of three each. The vocal gifts are those ministered by spoken words. The revelation gifts are those which are received by the mind being enlightened with spiritual thoughts that reveal certain things that are not made known by natural knowledge or wisdom. The third group consists of the power gifts, which demonstrate and minister the supernatural power of God.

The introductory Scripture (see 1 Cor. 12:7) to the gifts of the Spirit states that the manifestation of the Spirit is given to each one for the profit of all. *"For to one is given the word of wisdom by the Spirit, to another the word of knowledge through the same Spirit, to another faith by the same Spirit, to another gifts of healings by the same Spirit"* (1 Cor. 12:8-9). Please take note that everyone is given one or more, and they are all given the same way by the same Spirit.

The Pentecostals have taught that the gifts of the Spirit are for the Church today for more than one hundred years. Many books have been written on the gifts of the Spirit. I taught the gifts to students in a Pentecostal Bible college several decades ago. When I established the Christian International distance education college, I wrote a complete college course on the gifts of the Spirit, which is still available. Most books have a chapter devoted to each gift and give many Scriptures and scriptural examples of the gift in operation. There are also examples and illustrations from life experiences. However, we will look at just a few statements at this time to give the reader a basic understanding of the purpose and function of each gift.

THE SPIRITUAL GIFTS OF TONGUES AND INTERPRETATION OF TONGUES

The spiritual gift of tongues described in First Corinthians 12 does not serve the same purpose and ministry as the "other tongues" that a believer receives when he receives his personal gift of the Holy Spirit. All the gifts of the Spirit are for ministering to others. There are several applications and manifestations of this gift of tongues.

The most common is when a saint speaks out in tongues in a congregational setting. This is called a message in tongues. The complementary gift is the interpretation of tongues. The message in tongues is normally not in the language of the congregation, therefore the listeners do not understand what is being said. That is why the gift of tongues has to be accompanied by and work with the gift of interpretation of tongues. Apostle Paul dedicated the whole fourteenth chapter of First Corinthians to giving wisdom for the proper use of tongues in our personal lives and in local churches, such as how many messages in tongues should be given and who should interpret. He gave instructions for the proper use of prophecy and speaking in tongues. His summary statement in the last verse was, *"Therefore, brethren, desire earnestly to prophesy, and do not forbid the speaking with tongues"* (1 Cor. 14:39).

Giving messages in tongues in the church is still a valid ministry, if the interpretation is given. Paul advised his readers that it would be best not to allow more than three messages in tongues during one church service (see 1 Cor. 14:5). Also, if a person gives a message in tongues, he (or she) should not repeat it more than three times without it being interpreted. If no one present gives an interpretation and the Holy Spirit does not give it to the speaker of tongues, then he is not to continue speaking in tongues but to sit down and speak in tongues in his spirit and not speak out anymore during that service (see 1 Cor. 14:27-28). From my personal experience I can attest to the validity of Paul's advice to repeat a message in tongues a few times. During my early years in ministry when my children were small, I remember taking care of them when someone gave a message in tongues. The first time the message was given I was being distracted by my child and was not able to receive the interpretation. When the person gave it the second time, I was not being distracted and was able to clearly receive the interpretation and speak it forth. This allowed the congregation to understand the message and be blessed by it.

GIFTED WITH AN ETHNIC LANGUAGE

In the first few years after the original outpouring of the gift of the Holy Spirit during the Pentecostal Movement, there were frequent experiences of saints receiving the gifted ability to understand and speak in a human language they never learned. They usually felt that God had given them that language to become a missionary to the nation that spoke that language.

The first person to receive the gift of the Holy Spirit in Topeka, Kansas, spoke in the Chinese language, and later God gave her the ability to understand the language and communicate in Mandarin Chinese. Paul stated that a spirit language could be in the tongues of angels or men (an angelic language or a human language). Occasionally over the years, there have been testimonies of people present understanding the tongue that a newly baptized Christian was speaking. Sometimes this has also occurred with missionaries in a foreign land.

TONGUES: A SIGN TO UNBELIEVERS

Paul declared that tongues are for a sign, not to those who believe but to unbelievers. Paul based this on Isaiah's prophecy. *"…With men of other tongues and other lips I will speak to this people. And yet for all that they will not hear me, says the Lord"* (1 Cor. 14:21). When a sinner sees and hears his friend or relative speak in a language he knows that person has never learned, he can tell that something unusual and supernatural is happening.

ILLUSTRATED DURING ORIGINAL OUTPOURING

On the Day of Pentecost when all the believers were speaking in tongues, it was a sign to the Jews who had gathered from every nation. It caught their attention and drew them together. As the saints were praying in tongues, the presence of God was released and saturated the atmosphere over the people. Peter then preached in their Hebrew language about Jesus being their long-awaited Messiah. If they would repent and be baptized in the name of their Messiah—Jesus—then they would become candidates to receive the same gift the 120 had just received. The speaking in tongues was the starting point that resulted in 3,000 people getting saved.

A CONFIRMING TESTIMONY

John Sherrill wrote one of the first Charismatic books, called *They Speak With Other Tongues*. He gives a couple of instances to illustrate how tongues can be a positive sign to unbelievers:

> I recall several years ago when a certain man and woman were saved and baptized in the Spirit in a meeting where I was speaking. After the service they conferred with me about their concern for the salvation of their son, who had been with them on the previous Sunday. They informed me that he had violently opposed my message on the present day charismatic revival and the outpouring of the Holy Spirit. I had also observed this resistance as I preached. However, we agreed in prayer for his salvation. Two days later the young man sent word, asking if I would come to see him about an important matter. Upon my arrival I saw at once that a great change had taken place, for he was radiant and filled with joy.

> "Let me tell you what happened," he exclaimed. "I was alone in my room last night when the Lord began to deal with me about my spiritual condition convicting me of my sins. As a result, I have repented and given my heart to Jesus!" "Well, praise the Lord," I replied, inwardly thanking God for such a quick manifestation of the answer to our prayer of faith in his behalf.

And then what he said next was even more remarkable, for it revealed the unusual manner in which God had been able to reach him with the truth, although he had rejected the same Word when I had preached it the previous Sunday.

"The thing that really convinced me that there is something to all this," he continued, "is not only the wonderful change it has made in my mother's personality, but it was hearing her speak in new tongues. Why, she doesn't speak English grammatically correct, but you should hear her speak Hebrew by the Spirit!" (I had informed her that I had recognized her new tongue as Hebrew, as I used to teach Hebrew in the seminary.)

Then looking directly at me, he said: "The reason that I asked you to come to see me is that I too want to receive this experience which my mother and father have. Will you pray for me to receive the baptism in the Holy Spirit?" As I prayed for him, he began to speak in new tongues, worshiping the Lord as the Spirit gave him utterance. He had become saved and filled with the Spirit as a direct result of seeing and hearing the manifestation of tongues. It was a sign to him of the supernatural God at work convincing him of the truth *"Wherefore tongues are for a sign... to them that believeth not"* (1 Cor. 14:12).[1]

I will relate one other incident. Recently I prayed for a young woman to receive the baptism in the Holy Spirit where I was speaking, and she immediately began to speak in new tongues. A woman in the audience came up to her and said: "Here is my card. If you ever doubt that you spoke a true language by the Spirit, call me and I will tell you that I heard you speaking in Spanish, as I have studied the language. I have been on the fence about the baptism in the Holy Spirit, thinking perhaps there was nothing to it really, and that so-called speaking in tongues were just emotional gibberish—but let me tell you I am now fully convinced that all this is genuine!" The sign of tongues is still being used by the Spirit to convince the lost and convince the gainsayers of the validity of a supernatural, charismatic Christianity for this dispensation (see 1 Cor. 14:22).

CORPORATE PRAYING VS. PRIVATE PRAYING IN TONGUES

Paul explained that if all members of a church congregation pray in tongues for a long time and someone comes in, that person will think that the church people are out of their mind. But if just one speaks in tongues and another interprets it into the language of the people, or if one of the saints prophesies, then the visitor will be convinced that God is in their midst. He is convicted because he understands the words and the secrets of his heart are revealed, causing him to confess that the living God is truly in their midst (see 1 Cor. 14:25). That's why Paul stated that while he was speaking in a church service he would rather speak five words that the congregation could understand and be edified thereby than ten thousand words in other tongues that no one could understand (see 1 Cor. 14:19). However, Paul thanked God that in his personal prayer life he spoke in tongues more than anyone else (see 1 Cor. 14:18).

OUTWARDLY SPEAKING, BUT INWARDLY WORKING

Our individual gift of other tongues only works in us. Even when the spirit language is making intercession through us for others, it is working from within us. Though we are speaking out loud, it is still doing its work and ministry within our spirit man.

When we pray in tongues we are not praying to be heard of man but for God's hearing only. Anyhow, those present would not understand the words of our prayer, for we would be praying in our spirit language. Evangelicals think it brings confusion when everyone in a group prayer meeting begins praying in tongues. If we were praying to be heard of men, it would be confusion. But we are praying to God—who can hear millions of people praying at the same time and still know what each one is praying. After all, any time someone is praying, several hundreds of thousands, or even millions, of other believers around the world are praying at the same time.

NATURAL MAN DOES NOT UNDERSTAND SPIRITUAL THINGS

The gifts of giving a message in tongues and the interpretation of tongues can be activated by our prayer language because it puts us into the spirit realm where the gifts of the Spirit operate. Without a doubt, any Christian who has not received the gift that enables him to speak in other tongues would not be able to give a message in tongues. The same Spirit who gives us our spirit language gives the spiritual gifts, including the gift of tongues. This is almost impossible for the natural mind to comprehend for the Scripture says, *"The natural man does not receive the things of the Spirit of God, for they are foolishness to him; nor can he know them, because they are spiritually discerned"* (1 Cor. 2:14). The Living Bible says it like this, *"But the man who isn't a Christian cannot understand and can't accept these thoughts from God, which the Holy Spirit teaches us. They sound foolish to him, because only those who have the Holy Spirit within them can understand what the Holy Spirit means."*

I ministered with messages in tongues and gave interpretations while in my Pentecostal church. But when I started attending a restoration church where prophecy was the dominant gift being manifest, I started prophesying. The gift of tongues with the gift of interpretation of tongues ministers to the people in the same way that prophecy does. In churches where there is a strong ministry of prophesying, there are usually very few instances of tongues and interpretation manifested. Nevertheless, tongues and interpretation of tongues are still gifts that should be alive and active in the twenty-first century Church. And our spirit language still plays a vital role in the activation and operation of the gifts of the Spirit.

THE GIFT OF PROPHECY AND THE MINISTRY OF PROPHESYING

My primary ministry for fifty-eight years has been ministering with the gift of prophecy and prophesying as a prophet. Prophecy expresses the heart and mind of God. Scripture mentions five levels, or types, of prophecy: 1) the spirit of prophecy; 2) the spiritual gift of prophecy; 3) prophetic presbytery; 4) prophetic preaching; and 5) the office of a prophet. (Please see my book *Prophets and Personal Prophecy* for a complete presentation of all five levels of prophetic ministry with guidelines for properly giving and receiving personal prophecies.[2])

The first level of prophesying is that which all saints can do. This is the type of prophesying that Paul was speaking of when he said, *"You may all prophesy one by one"* (1 Cor. 14:31). Revelation 19:10 calls it *"the spirit of prophecy which is the testimony of Jesus."* If Jesus wants to express or share something with one of His children, He uses the spirit of prophecy. The many ministers affiliated with Christian International and I have activated and trained over 250,000 Christians to minister in this order of prophesying.

As those who are activated continue to grow in the prophetic ministry, it will be discovered and determined whether the Holy Spirit has given them the spiritual gift of prophecy, which is the second level of prophesying. Paul exhorted those who had the ministry of prophesying to prophesy according to the proportion of their faith (see Rom. 12:6). Some may even be called to the fivefold ascension office of a prophet. Regardless of which level of prophecy a person is ministering on, praying in tongues plays an important role in enabling him or her to function in prophetic ministry to bless others.

As described in Chapter 4, in 1973 I had a sovereign visitation from God and started prophesying to hundreds of individuals in one setting. Any time I would begin to feel spiritually low, tired, or that the prophetic word was not coming clearly, I would pray for a minute or so in tongues to recharge my spiritual battery and clear my spiritual perception. If I feel the Lord is leading me to minister in the power gifts, then I usually take an hour or two to power up ahead of time by praying in the Holy Ghost with my spirit prayer language. I have witnessed thousands of people being empowered by praying in tongues—which has proven to me that praying in the spirit performs all the blessings we are sharing in this book. The Holy Spirit really knew what He was doing when He chose the spirit language as the greatest gift He could give to the believer. Let us show great appreciation for His gift by giving maximum time to praying in our spirit prayer language.

THE GIFT OF WORD OF KNOWLEDGE

There are three kinds of knowledge: natural learned knowledge, divine biblical knowledge, and the gift of the word of knowledge. Divine knowledge can be gained by studying the Word of God and receiving divine illumination for proper understanding and application. The word of knowledge is a gift that is given by the Spirit of the Lord. It involves knowing facts about people and circumstances that the person did not receive by natural knowledge. It is seeing, hearing, or sensing things by the Spirit. The word of knowledge gives knowledge about things that existed in the past or exist in the present.

God gave Elijah a word of knowledge that there were 7,000 Israelites who had not bowed their knees to Baal (see 1 Kings 19:18). It was a word of knowledge that made Elisha know the plans that the king of Samaria would make in his private war rooms (see 2 Kings 6:9). By the word of knowledge Jesus knew that the Samaritan woman at the well had been married to five husbands and the man she was living with was not her husband (see John 4:16-19). Scripture is full of additional examples of the word of knowledge.

A word of knowledge can reveal certain physical conditions that need to be healed. When a person ministers in the Spirit by saying that someone is present with this or that condition, or calling forth those who are going through a certain thing, it is the word of knowledge giving them that information. The word of knowledge works much in prophetic ministry. It is a thin line at times between a prophetic revelation and a word of knowledge.

The Scriptures emphatically emphasize that all the gifts are given by the same Spirit. There is no implication that some of the gifts are greater or lesser, or that it requires more of the Spirit to manifest some gift more than others. The same four principles are involved in activating and ministering the gifts. The same spirit language can activate and empower saints to minister the gifts of the Spirit. Remember, the Holy Spirit did not give all the gifts to every believer, but He did give every believer the one gift that can activate and give empowerment for the manifestation of any and all the gifts the Holy Spirit has distributed to them. *"The Holy Spirit distributes gifts to individuals as He wills." "It is the same and only Holy Spirit who gives all these gifts and powers, deciding which each one of us should have"* (1 Cor. 12:11 TLB).

THE GIFT OF THE WORD OF WISDOM

The word of wisdom reveals some of the future happenings, Ministry, and prophetic purposes of God in an individual's life.

Where the word of knowledge speaks of the past and present, the word of wisdom speaks mostly of the future. It also sometimes gives words of wisdom on how to handle present situations. In giving more than 50,000 individuals personal prophecies over fifty-eight years of ministry, I have noticed a certain pattern the Holy Spirit follows. The personal prophecy will normally speak first of things the individual has experienced in the past and some of what they are facing and going through in the present. I have discovered the Holy Spirit does that to let the person witness that the prophetic word about their past and present is accurate so that their faith is built to accept and believe that the words about their future are accurate and will come to pass.

Your inner, born-of-the-Spirit, baptized-in-the-Holy-Spirit being knows all the gifts and ministries that have been distributed to you. Your spirit language prays for those gifts to be activated. The spirit language empowers and enlightens the mind of the believer with the word of wisdom to minister to others.

DISCERNING OF SPIRITS

There are only three sources of spirit activity or types of spirit beings: God and His heavenly spirit beings, Satan and his demonic spirits, and human spirits—humankind spirit beings who are clothed with flesh and bone bodies. God and His heavenly spirit beings are always good and holy. Satan and his fallen angels and evil spirits are always bad and evil. Man's spirit is neutral, but becomes either good or bad based on whether the spirit of man is being influenced by the devil's evil spirit or God's Holy Spirit.

The spiritual gift of discerning of spirits is able to discern which spirit is motivating the words or actions of a person. Often it can discern what evil spirits are inhabiting a person. It can also discern the good spirits that are within a person (see Mark 9:17, 23). It is an operation of the Spirit and therefore can be activated by one's spirit language, especially if discerning of spirits is one of the gifts of the Spirit that has been distributed to the believer. Discerning of spirits is not the gift of human suspicion or judging human fleshly manifestations.

THE GIFT OF FAITH

A saint or fivefold minister who has been given the gift of faith can perform miracles as easily as a person with the gift of prophecy can prophesy. The gift of faith enables a person to believe for the impossible. It gives a person the supernatural heart assurance and confidence that when they speak the word, it will happen. The gift of faith works mainly in miraculous healings, deliverance from demonic activity, and great faith for finances.

There are three levels or realms of faith: saving faith for salvation, the fruit of the Spirit of faith, and the gift of faith that is one of the gifts of the Spirit. Saving faith has to come from the heart/spirit of a person, while the fruit of faith and the gift of faith come from the Holy Spirit. All levels require a Spirit activation and operation. Praying in our spirit language is an activator of the spirit of man and the Spirit of God. Praying in tongues can activate the gift of faith in those who have been given this gift.

WORKING OF MIRACLES

This gift works miracles in creation by superseding the ordinary course of nature. Aaron's rod blossoming and growing almonds overnight was a manifestation of the working of miracles (see Num. 17:8). Also, the Red Sea parting and Balaam's donkey speaking were miracles. Elijah and Elisha worked miracles, such as one pint of oil filling many containers with gallons of oil (see 2 Kings 4:1-7). Jesus turned water into wine, walked on water, and fed 5,000 with one small basket of bread and fish, all of which are demonstrations of the working of miracles (see John 6:5-14; Matt. 14:28; John 2:5-11).

The Greek words for "working of miracles" are *energema* and *dunamis*. *Dunamis* is the same word translated as "power" in Acts 1:8. *Dunamis* of the Spirit is produced the same way electrical power is produced in a hydroelectric plant. The water going through the water gate turns a turbine that causes the rotation of a dynamo in the heart of the dam that produces electrical power. Remember the illustration in Chapter 5: the water is the river of life flowing out of our innermost being, the water gate is our mouth, and the turbine is our tongue. Speaking in tongues turns the Holy Spirit dynamo in our spirit that generates the *dunamis* power of God. Speaking in our spirit language definitely can produce the *dunamis* power for the working of miracles.

GIFTS OF HEALINGS

Both words are plural, *"to another gifts of healings by the same Spirit"* (1 Cor. 12:9). Please take note that this is the only gift with this uniqueness. This reveals that there may be saints who receive a special gift of healing for specific diseases and sicknesses. It is like the modern medical field where most doctors specialize in one particular area of physical problems. There may be as many specialty gifts as there are special needs in the human body. I have seen this proven true in my fifty-eight years of ministry and in studying the ministry of great healing ministers of the past.

For example, I have known ministers who had a gift of healing for cancers so that almost everyone with a cancerous problem for whom they prayed was healed. Yet, that same person could pray for someone with a headache and not see any healing take place. One translation says, *"You who have the gift of healing heal the sick"* (1 Cor. 12:9 TLB), which would apply more to one's specialty gift of healing. When ministers who have discovered and proven their special anointed gifts of healing are holding a healing service, they will often call forth the people with that problem first and pray for them. As those people are miraculously healed, it builds faith and expectation in others for God to heal them of their conditions.

God brings healing to people's physical bodies in several ways. Natural healing occurs when a doctor—or someone else—removes the cause of the problem and then the body heals itself. Individual healing occurs by a person exercising personal faith for his or her healing. The prayer of faith by the church elders also brings divine healing (see James 5:14, 15). Then there is the Holy Spirit's gifts of healings that can remove the problem and result in a progressive full healing, which means that the body recovers fully over time. The gifts of healings can also produce an instantaneous healing and restoration back to normal function.

If every saint only received one gift of the Spirit, instead of several, and they were equally distributed, then every ninth saint would have a gift of healing. That gift should be activated and used to heal saints in the Church, as well as used in prophetic evangelism to heal sinners so that they experience the goodness of God and repent (see Rom. 2:4).

ALL GIFTS GIVEN BY GOD'S GRACE— BUT RECEIVED AND ACTIVATED BY MAN'S FAITH

The gifts of the Spirit have been restored to the Church and they are being activated into manifestation by those who know how to fully use their spirit languages and practice the four principles for the activation of their spiritual gifts.

All nine manifestations or gifts of the Holy Spirit are distributed to the saints according to God's predestined knowledge of each saint's ability to manifest certain gifts. The Holy Spirit not only gives the believer the gift of his spirit language, but He also gives certain of the nine gifts to every Spirit-baptized child of God. First Corinthians 12:7 emphatically declares, *"The manifestation of the Spirit is given to each one for the profit of all."*

The gifts are not temporarily loaned to the person; they are given. They become a part of one's new born-again spirit being, just like the gift of eternal life and the gift of the Holy Spirit. Just like talking in tongues becomes an ability of a saint's spirit, the saint's gifts of the Holy Spirit become a divine ability of his new creation, inner man, who has been given this supernatural gifted ability. That does not mean that the gifts automatically manifest because they have been given. The believer has to receive revelation that the gifts are within him and then has to operate his faith to activate the gifts into manifestation. The Holy Spirit's gift of the believer's spirit language is the great activator. Praying in tongues produces the fruit of faith, which is the level of faith needed to believe for the gifts to be manifested.

Praying in tongues is like the car key that starts the engine with its pistons, which make the engine produce the power that gets the car moving. Our spirit language is the pony motor that activates the big engine of the powerful Caterpillar™. Praying in tongues is the turbine turning until it activates the dynamo that produces the electrical power that makes the lights shine and the big engines produce great works. Our sprit language is one of the major keys to the Kingdom of God that Jesus said He would give to His Church. It is the great motivator, Generator, and activator of all God's grace and gifts in our lives. The Holy Spirit knew all of this when He chose the gifted ability of speaking in unknown tongues with our spirit language as the greatest gift that He could give to the individual members of Christ's corporate Body, the Church.

GRIEVE NOT THE HOLY SPIRIT!

(See Eph. 4:30; 1 Thess. 5:19.)

How grieved the Holy Spirit must be with us when we do not use the gift He has given to us to grow His fruit and manifest His gifts. But how thrilled Jesus must be when we receive the Holy

Spirit, since He died and rose again in order to send the Holy Spirit to His people still on earth. Christ Jesus is also very pleased when His saints receive the Holy Spirit's gift of the spirit language. And the whole Godhead rejoices when we receive and manifest the greatest gift each gave for humankind to be children of God, to live the life of Christ, and to do the works that Jesus did and even greater works. The most fulfilling of all for Jesus is seeing His children maturing and being conformed to His image until His Church can be presented unto Him as a glorious Bride, without spot or wrinkle, ready to rule and reign with Him for evermore (see Eph.4:26-27; Rev. 5:10; Rom. 8:17).

70 REASONS CONTINUED...

FORTY-ONE

The gifts of eternal life and the spirit language are given for our own edification and benefit. However, the gifts of the Spirit are given to believers to meet the needs of others. They are the nine manifestations of the Spirit. The gifts demonstrate that our God and Savior Jesus Christ is alive and active in the world today. The three vocal gifts demonstrate that God speaks to and through His people. The three revelation gifts reveal that our God is omniscient—knowing all things about everything and everyone, and He reveals some of those things to His people. The three power gifts reveal that our God is omnipotent and demonstrates His power over demons, humankind, and nature. Praying in tongues is a power plant within producing the faith needed to manifest the gifts of the Spirit (see Rom. 6:23; 1 Cor. 12:7-12; 14:2; Jude 1:20).

FORTY-TWO

Speaking in tongues in our personal spirit language is a different gift operation and serves a different purpose than the gift of tongues, which is one of the nine gifts of the Spirit. By the restoration and demonstration of the gift of "different kinds of tongues" in the Pentecostal Movement, we understand it to be a "message in tongues" given for the benefit of others when accompanied with the sister gift of interpretation of tongues (see 1 Cor. 14:26-28).

FORTY-THREE

Speaking in tongues can also serve as a sign to unbelievers. This is especially true when a believer speaks in a language that he does not understand, but that is understood by someone present. Numerous testimonies have been given of this happening, and it usually results in someone accepting Christ or being convinced that speaking in tongues is a supernatural gift of God. "Tongues" may be an earth language or heavenly language (see 1 Cor. 13:1; 14:22).

FORTY-FOUR

Our spirit language was given to empower us to manifest the gifts of the Spirit. The gifts are not loaned, but are given to believers. All nine gifts are in the Holy Spirit, who is in us. However, only certain gifts are given to each believer as a part of the ability of our individual spirit being. They become the characteristics and capability of our new creation man in Christ Jesus. The Holy Spirit distributes the gifts to individuals according to the foreknowledge and will of God. He knows the DNA of each member, his or her position and ministry in His corporate Body, and what gifts each member was given the potential to manifest. As a member of the Body of Christ they become our unique membership ministry manifestation. The manifestation of the Spirit is given to everyone for the profit of others. The Holy Spirit also has given the believer a spirit language to bring that potential to productivity and manifestation. The ministry of the spirit language activating the nine gifts of the Spirit gives us nine more major reasons for praying in tongues (see 1 Cor. 12:7, 11, 18, 27).

SEVENTY REASONS FOR SPEAKING IN TONGUES

FORTY-FIVE

The benefits of speaking in tongues have been proven by the experience of millions over the last one hundred years. I have seen it proven thousands of times during my sixty years of being Spirit-baptized and ministering my spirit language and gifts of the Holy Spirit. Praying in tongues definitely does empower Christians to receive and manifest all the gifts and ministries of the Holy Spirit. The Holy Spirit really knew what He was doing when He chose the spirit language as the greatest gift He could give to the believer. Let us show great appreciation for His gift by giving maximum time to praying in our spirit prayer language. "Thanks be to God for His unspeakable gift" or the gift that cannot be spoken with one's learned language (see 2 Cor. 9:15; Col. 2:7).

FORTY-SIX

The Bible says to Christians, *"Forbid not to speak with tongues," "do not quench the Spirit"* and *"do not grieve the Holy Spirit."* When we refuse to receive the Holy Spirit's gift of speaking in tongues it quenches and grieves the Spirit. How grieved the Holy Spirit must also be when we who have received do not use the spirit language gift He has given us to grow His fruit and manifest His gifts. But how thrilled Jesus must be when we receive and use the greatest gift that was given by God the Father, Jesus Christ and the Holy Spirit. They all know the spirit language is the key to utilizing and activating all the benefits and ministries that have been given to the saints. The spirit language is one of the major "keys to the kingdom of Heaven" that Jesus promised to give to His disciples (see 1 Cor. 14:39; 1 Thess. 5:19; Eph. 4:30; Matt. 16:19).

ENDNOTES

1. John Sherrill, *They Speak With Other Tongues* (Fleming H. Revell Company, 1977).

2. Bill Hamon, *Prophets and Personal Prophecy* (Shippensburg, PA: Destiny Image, 1987).

CHAPTER 9

THE HOLY SPIRIT'S "GIFT"—HELPER AND WARRIOR MAKER

THE HOLY SPIRIT—THE HELPER

A HELPER, NOT A DICTATOR

Jesus prophetically promised His followers that He would send them another Helper. John recorded that Jesus gave this promise four times (see John 14:16, 25; 15:26; 16:7). Other translations use different words to describe what Jesus would send, such as Counselor, Comforter, advocate, another to befriend you, and someone else to stand by you.[1] I use the New King James Version as my personal Bible. It translates the Greek word *parakletos* as "Helper," and this word best describes the main work of the Holy Spirit that I want to explain and emphasize in this chapter. When the Holy Spirit came He manifested His presence by enabling each person to speak in a new language of the Spirit. As we have seen, the ability to speak in an unknown tongue with a spirit language is the evidence that a person has received the gift of the Holy Spirit.

WHAT IS THE GIFT?

We now want to discover what the gift is. The Holy Spirit is not a dictator over the believer, but a Helper. In my early

Pentecostal days the Holy Spirit was perceived as a dictator in regard to manifesting the blessings and works of the Spirit. The belief was that nothing could be manifest unless the Spirit sovereignly willed it, timed it, controlled, and directed it. This was believed to be true concerning speaking in tongues, manifesting the gifts of the Spirit, and certain ways we praised the Lord. When such an experience came forth it was usually based on having a strong emotional motivation and action that was supposed to be the Holy Spirit moving without any of the will or faith of the Christian being involved.

An example of this is what we called "dancing in the Spirit." I experienced "dancing in the Spirit" three times before I became a pastor. It was not considered an act of the will to praise God as it is today. It was seen as a time when the Holy Spirit took complete control of one's body and made the person dance, usually a very wild uncontrolled dance. My three experiences of dancing and then falling down under the power were somewhat typical of the practice. The first time was at a little Assembly of God church in Boswell, Oklahoma, which I attended for nine months after I got saved and received the gift of the Holy Spirit in July of 1950 at age sixteen. I was praising the Lord with several others when suddenly I felt as if an electrical current had started ascending up my legs. When it hit my knees I started dancing and twirling about like a white tornado. I danced from the front of the church to the back knocking chairs in both directions and making a new aisle in the church.

The second time was at an evangelistic meeting. This time I twirled about and then seemed to float down to the floor. A similar experience happened in Bible college. But the Bible college was a restoration college that taught that we are to deliberately do acts of faith in expressing our joyful praise to God and manifesting the gifts of the Spirit.

After leaving Bible college, I started pastoring a church in February 1954 at age nineteen. A month later I invited an evangelist to hold a series of meetings for the church. One night God's Spirit moved with a flow of worship that lasted for almost two hours. Many in the Church were praising God in the dance.

I had moved off the platform to join them down front. I was dancing a worshipful dance and felt like I was dancing with Jesus or an angel. It was smooth and flowing.

After dancing in this manner for about twenty minutes I began to sense it was time for a change in the order of the service. But I was in a dilemma as to how to do that. I was down front and not behind the pulpit. And besides, I was "dancing in the Spirit" with my eyes shut. The belief was that to be "in the Spirit" one must keep his (or her) eyes shut and not indicate that he is having anything to do with what was happening—except allowing the Spirit to have His way. According to my past experiences and the tradition of the church, I couldn't just stop, open my eyes, and walk back upon the platform. If I did, it would look like I left being in the Spirit and moved "in the flesh."

In my zeal to do what was right, be spiritual, and end this dancing like it ended in the past, I decided I would need to twirl about and allow the Holy Spirit to gently lay me down on the cement floor. So I started twirling, let out a loud shout, and then fell backward—onto the cement floor. After regaining consciousness, I lay there a few minutes. Later people told me that when I fell it sounded like a sack of potatoes being dropped from the ceiling and hitting the floor. The scream and sound of the fall caused everyone to immediately stop what they were doing and look about. The evangelist told everyone to lift their hands, close their eyes, and praise the Lord. He then quickly left the platform and came to where I was and felt my pulse to see if I was still alive. He then went back to the pulpit and told them everything was fine, that I was just out in the Spirit.

Now, I was in a greater dilemma than I had been before. I thought I would get up anyhow, but as I rolled my head to the other side it raised up about two inches, and when I started to lift my head my hair was sticking to the floor! I knew then that I had a big knot on the back of my head and that it was bleeding. The custom was that if you were really in the Spirit then you would not be hurt when falling under the power. I felt that if I got up at that point everyone would assume that I had been in the flesh. So I laid there and rolled my head back and forth hoping to roll that knot out before the people could see it. I could tell my head was lying next to the platform and any blood would flow under the platform (I had cleaned the church before and knew the floor sloped that direction). I lay there until the evangelist finished preaching and praying for people and everyone left—except for three people who would end up being my wife, her mother, and her best friend.

I learned a vital lesson that evening about making a transition into new spiritual revelation and ways of demonstrating the Spirit. We can get in the flesh while trying to be spiritual, especially when God is transitioning us to His new order of worship and ways of manifesting the Spirit. God was transitioning me from Pentecostal "dancing in the Spirit" to the Latter Rain worship and praise that I had begun experiencing in February 1952.

Just four months after this dancing experience, in July 1954, I attended a Restoration Conference in North Surrey, British Columbia. That was the place and time when a sovereign visitation of God came and liberated and activated everyone into the new order of praise in the dance. The description of that restoration visitation is described on page 232 in my book *The Eternal Church*. I shared this experience to show that the Holy Spirit was not sent to dominate, control, or force us to manifest the Spirit. The Holy Spirit was not sent to be a dictator but our Helper. Jesus said He would send "the Helper" not "the Forceful Controller" or the "Independent Spirit" who has to be talked into helping.

THE GIFT: THE HELPER WHO HELPS

The Living Webster Encyclopedic Dictionary of the English Language[2] describes Helper as "one who helps," and to help is "to provide assistance, to cooperate with, to benefit, to be of use in providing a remedy." The Holy Spirit was sent by Christ to work with His Church. The Spirit is committed to helping all members of the Body of Christ fulfill and accomplish all that God has called them to be and do. The Helper, whom Jesus sent, is One who assists and cooperates with Christians who are seeking to accomplish a work of God. All the resources of God's love, wisdom, and power are with the Holy Spirit. And He is with us and has given us the gift that enables us to access and activate all those resources.

The Spirit is more desirous and willing to manifest God's power in and through us than we are to receive and manifest God's grace and gifts. Though I know this is biblically true, yet it is hard for me to grasp that it is an actual fact, especially when I think about the amount of desire and passion I have to manifest Jesus as the only true and all powerful God. If we really understood and believed who the Holy Spirit is, then our faith would increase tremendously to receive, believe, and manifest the gifts of God. We must act upon Jesus' admonition concerning our desires: *"What things soever ye desire, when ye pray, believe that ye receive them, and ye shall have them"* (Mark 11:24 KJV). We must add the faith that receives, then we will possess and demonstrate all that the Holy Spirit has for us.

The Spirit is our Helper. He is ready and willing twenty-four hours a day to assist us and cooperate with us to accomplish God's purpose. God knows that He can do exceedingly, abundantly above all we can ask or think, but He also knows that it has to be according to the power that is working within us. The Holy Spirit expects us to use the gift of our spirit language to generate that "power within us" which is needed for God to do those exceeding and abundant things for us (see Eph. 3:20).

THE BANK ACCOUNT EXAMPLE

One translation (see John 14:16 PNT) conveys the idea that "the Helper" stands alongside our spirit with all the provisions needed to enable us to fulfill our ministry. Remember the analogy from Chapter 5 of Jesus putting a million dollars into our bank account, with all of it being available for us to write as many checks as needed to meet our personal needs and the needs of God's people? If we only wrote five and ten dollar checks now and then, we would be counted very foolish and fearful or lacking the vision and desire to write bigger checks more often to accomplish more. Most Christians do not use their checkbook, which is their spirit language, to write multiple or large checks on their fully loaded bank account, which is the Holy Spirit. Jesus deposited into the Holy Spirit all that we would ever need to excel exceedingly abundantly in glorifying God and ministering to humankind.

GOD'S WILL—MAN'S FAITH

Prior to the Charismatic Movement, it was taught that the Holy Spirit only manifests the gifts of the Spirit according to His own will. Back then we received the impression from our teachers that the Spirit was reluctant and indifferent about manifesting the gifts of the Spirit. Sometimes He was willing to manifest His gifts, and sometimes He wasn't in the mood. Therefore, there was nothing that saints could do to manifest the gifts but to wait until the Spirit was willing.

This teaching generally came from a wrong interpretation and application of First Corinthians 12:11. After listing the nine gifts of the Holy Spirit in the previous three verses and emphasizing that they are all given the same way by the same Spirit, Paul declared that *"one and the same Spirit works all these things, distributing to each one individually as He wills."* Please note that *"as He wills"* is in relation to the distribution of the gifts to different individuals and not in relation to the saints manifesting the gifts. Every gift of God is given, but must be received and manifested by the faith of the believer. The gift of eternal life is received and lived by faith. The gift of the Holy Spirit is received by faith. The believer who receives the gift speaks in tongues by faith. The gifts of the Spirit are received and manifested by faith. Every gift of God is by grace and faith. God's grace is His unmerited love and power that makes the gift available to whosoever will believe and receive. By God's grace we are saved through our faith. That is why we developed the following statement and use it when teaching saints how to appropriate and activate the gifts of the Spirit: *Gifts are given by the sovereign will of God, but they are activated and manifested by the faith of the believer!*

God gives the gift, but each believer must receive it into his or her life by faith. God so loved the world that He gave the gift of His Son, but the world must receive the gift of His Son to have God's gift of everlasting life. The same is true for the gift of the Holy Spirit and the gifts of the Spirit. We have shown in other chapters how praying in our spirit language is the main means by which we can activate and manifest the supernatural works of God and the gifts of the Spirit.

SPIRIT LANGUAGE—THE WARRIOR MAKER

THE WARRIOR NATURE OF THE GODHEAD

Our spirit language takes on the same nature as the Holy Spirit who gave it to us. The Holy Spirit has the same nature as Christ Jesus who sent Him. Jesus has the same nature of Almighty God. God is a Mighty Warrior. One of the major characteristics of the nature of the Godhead is that of a Mighty Warrior. Several places in Scripture state that God fought for Israel.

In the tenth chapter of Joshua is the story of Joshua and his army battling against the army of five kings in Canaan. Joshua was fulfilling God's command for him to kill every human in the land of Canaan and possess it for the nation of Israel. God had been helping from the unseen realm by enabling Joshua's army to be mighty, victorious warriors.

GOD PERSONALLY JOINS THE BATTLE

Joshua and his Israelite army would battle for seven years before destroying enough of the inhabitants of the land of Canaan for it to become the nation of Israel. But this particular battle against the five Amorite kings would be different, for God Himself would personally get involved in the battle. As God intently watched Joshua fighting and conquering His enemies, His warrior nature was so stirred within Him that it motivated Him to personally participate.

God suddenly commanded Archangel Michael, His general over the armies of Heaven, to bring from His war room some of His hailstone bullets and bombs. Almighty God took some of the bombs in His hand and threw them at the enemy killing thousands. He kept throwing His hailstone bombs until he had killed the majority of the enemy soldiers. After the battle He commissioned the Holy Spirit to make sure it was recorded that, *"There were more who died from the hailstones than the children of Israel killed with the sword"* (Josh. 10:11). The Lord wanted all to know that He was a Warrior and the mightiest of all warriors. Our Lord Jesus Christ is not only the King of all kings, He is also the Warrior of all warriors. Exodus 15:3 declares, *"The LORD is a man of war."* Other translations of that verse state: *"The LORD is a warrior;" "Yahweh is a warlike one;" "The LORD—the warrior*

God;" "Jehovah is mighty in battle;" and *"The Eternal knows well how to fight."*[3]

GREATEST MIRACLE GIVEN FOR KILLING ENEMIES

There have been many great miracles in God's natural creation. The great flood of Noah's day covered the earth with water. The Red Sea was divided, as was the Jordan River. Jesus walked on water and fed 5,000 people with a handful of food. These miracles, and others, are well-known. But people are often shocked when I teach that the greatest recorded miracle in nature happened in order for God's soldiers to have more time to kill their enemies.

Joshua spoke to the sun and moon to stand still and not move—and they obeyed. Time stood still for almost twenty-four hours to give more daylight time for Joshua to finish destroying those whom he had been commissioned to dispossess. Joshua 10:14 summarizes what happened that day, *"And there has been no day like that, before it or after it, that the Lord heeded the voice of a man; for the Lord fought for Israel."* God fought two ways. First, He fought as a Mighty Warrior killing Amorites. Second, when Joshua commanded time to go on pause until he had the opportunity to finish killing his enemies, God fought as the Almighty Creator of Heaven and earth. God fought by superseding the laws He established in His original creation. He established time by the rotation of the earth, sun, solar system, and universe. The Creator who started time can also stop time and still continue everything working for humankind on earth. His wisdom and power held everything in order for almost a whole day.

God also stirred up His warrior nature and personally fought and killed thousands of the army of the Amorites. These are the same Amorites that God was referring to when He told Abraham that he and his descendants could not possess the land of Canaan until the sin of the Amorites was full (see Gen. 15:16). By Joshua's time, the cup of iniquity of the Amorites had become full to overflowing. So Joshua was in the land of Canaan executing the judgments written against them, so that God's people could possess their promised land and become their own sovereign nation (see Ps. 149:6-9).

SPIRIT LANGUAGE—THE WARRIOR MAKER

Our spirit language from the Holy Spirit takes on the same warrior nature of the Godhead. Praying in the Spirit with our spirit language is a vital part of the Christian armor. Apostle Paul described the different parts of the war armor for a Christian soldier: for his head, the helmet of salvation; for his chest and back, the breastplate of righteousness; for his waist, the belt of truth; for his feet, the combat boots of the preparation of the Gospel of peace; for his fighting arms and hands, the shield of faith in one hand and the sword of the Spirit, which is the Word of God, in the other hand. And praying in the spirit language, which is the inner power producer empowering the Christian soldier with the will, wisdom, courage, and power to fight the good fight of faith (see Eph. 6:10-18).

Finally, my brethren, be strong in the Lord and the power of His might. Put on the whole armor of God that you may be able to stand against the wiles of the devil. For we do not wrestle against flesh and blood, but against principalities, against powers, against the rulers of the darkness of this age, and against spiritual hosts of wickedness in the heavenly places (see Eph. 6:10-12).

For though we walk in the flesh, we do not war according to the flesh. For the weapons of our warfare are not carnal but mighty in God for pulling down strongholds of evil (2 Corinthians 10:3-4).

WARRING WITH OUR SPIRIT LANGUAGE AGAINST EVIL SPIRIT FORCES

Christian warfare is in the spiritual realm. We do not battle against flesh and bone humans, but against spirit beings and demonic spirits that function in the spirit realm. It is sometimes referred to as our warfare in the heavenlies. There are three realms of the "heavenlies." The first heaven is the natural atmosphere around the earth. The third heaven is where God sits on His throne ruling over everything. The second heaven is the space between earth's atmosphere and the outer perimeter of the third heaven. The devil and all his fallen angels and demonic spirits operate from the headquarters of hell in the heart of the earth to the second heaven.

As saints, we are to fight with our spiritual weapons from our spiritual position. That position is where Christ raised us up and positioned us for battle: *"God raised us up together, and made us sit together in the heavenly places in Christ Jesus"* (Eph. 2:6). Where are these heavenly places where the saints are positioned? We need to know our place and power. Apostle Paul prayed to God the Father of our Lord Jesus Christ for the saints to receive the spirit of wisdom and revelation for this purpose:

> *...that the God of our Lord Jesus Christ, the Father of glory, may give to you the spirit of wisdom and revelation in the knowledge of Him, the eyes of your understanding being enlightened; that you may know what is the hope of His calling, what are the riches of the glory of His inheritance in the saints, and what is the exceeding greatness of His power toward us who believe, according to the working of His mighty power which He worked in Christ when He raised Him from the dead and seated Him at His right hand in the heavenly places, far above all principality and power and might and dominion, and every name that is named, not only in this age but also in that which is to come.*

> *And He put all things under His feet, and gave Him to be head over all things to the church, which is His body, the fullness of Him who fills all in all* (Ephesians 1:17-23).

Blessed be the God and Father of our Lord Jesus Christ who has blessed us with every spiritual blessing in the heavenly places in Christ (Ephesians 1:3). The fellowship of the mystery...that now the manifold wisdom of God might be made known by the church to the principalities and powers in the heavenly places, according to the eternal purpose which He accomplished in Christ Jesus our Lord (Ephesians 3:9-11).

WARRIOR SAINTS HEADQUARTERS AND COMMAND CENTER

As saints of God, our position in our spirit life is in the heavenly places in Christ who is seated at the right hand of God. This means we operate from the realm of the third heaven where Jesus Christ is seated at the right hand of Almighty God and where we are seated in Christ Jesus. Our position is

"And what is the exceeding greatness of His power toward us who believe, according to the working of His mighty power which He worked in Christ when He raised Him from the dead and seated Him at His right hand in the heavenly places, far above all principality and power and might and dominion, and every name that is named, not only in this age but also in that which is to come. And He put all things under His feet, and gave Him to be head over all things to the church, which is His body, the fullness of Him who fills all in all" (Ephesians 1:19-23).

Praying in our spirit language activates us into our heavenly place. It is a mystery and a paradox that we can be living in the natural world, walking and talking in our natural body, and yet at the same time in our spirit we can be seated at the right hand of God in Christ Jesus.

THE SAINTS' GARDEN OF EDEN

Adam and Eve had a Garden of Eden where everything was available that they would need to do the work of God. As saints, we have our own Garden of Eden. It is called the heavenly places in Christ Jesus. Our Lord Jesus Christ has provided and *"blessed us with every spiritual blessing in the heavenly places in Christ"* (Eph. 1:3).

Adam and Eve had to stay in the Garden to have all those blessings available. We have to stay in the heavenly places in Christ to participate and demonstrate Christ's life and supernatural works. That is the reason the Bible tells us to walk in the Spirit, live in the Spirit, and pray in the Spirit. The main way we pray in the Spirit is to pray in the spirit language with which the Holy Spirit has gifted us. The spirit language opens the gate to our Garden of Eden and then directs us to the resources and helps us appropriate all we need to accomplish God's purpose for our lives. Our authority and position is above all of the activity of the devil and all of his host of fallen angels and demons, who are limited mainly to the first realm of the heavenlies above and to their fiery hell below.

THE SAINTS' POSITION AND WEAPONS

All evil forces are under our feet. When we function out of our place of being hidden with Christ in God, we have power over the devil's entire host. Our battle is not with flesh and blood beings, but we do battle against evil spirit beings. Our warfare is not with carnal earthly weapons, but we are in war and we have been given mighty spiritual weapons to pull down the stronghold of hell.

The major weapons of warfare for the Church are the blood of Jesus, the name of Jesus Christ, the Word of God, the high praises of God, the shout of faith, the gifts of the Spirit, and the spirit language which empowers the saints with the love, faith, and power to use these weapons effectively.

LUCIFER CAST OUT OF THIRD HEAVEN

War broke out in heaven: Michael and his war angels fought with the dragon and the dragon and his angels fought. But they did not prevail, nor was a place found for them in heaven any longer. So the great dragon was cast out, that serpent of old, called the Devil and Satan, who deceives the whole world; he was cast to the earth, and his angels were cast out with him (Revelation 12:7-9).

This is a prophetic account of what happened in the original rebellion of Lucifer and what will take place in the near future when Satan and all his followers will be cast from earth's atmosphere and into the lake of fire. Michael and God's holy angels cast Lucifer out of Heaven, but Jesus and His army of saints will fight against him and cast them off the earth and into the lake of fire (see Rev. 19:11-21).

Rebellious Lucifer and his fallen angels were cast out of Third Heaven to the first heaven around the earth. The fall of Lucifer caused great catastrophic eruptions to earth, resulting in the earth becoming without form and void (see Gen. 1:2). The earth was covered with water and God removed all light from reaching earth, which caused it to be plunged into total darkness and frozen into one big ball of ice.

When God started fixing the earth back up for human habitation, He had to brood over the frozen waters with the warmth of His light. It was the third day of His creative work before the frozen water around the earth was melted enough for God to separate the earth into dry land and waters of rivers, lakes, and oceans. The remaining three days God created all creatures for the air, waters, and land. His last creative act was the creation of man in His own image and likeness. The eight major reasons for God creating man from the earth and making earth his home are covered thoroughly in my book titled, *Who Am I and Why Am I Here?*[4]

MAN MADE MIGHTIER THAN THE DEVIL

Humankind is the only creation of God that was made in God's own image and likeness. Lucifer was not made in God's image and likeness. Lucifer was one of God's archangels and was originally His minister of music. Lucifer fell and became the devil, who is the originator and god of all evil and everything that is contrary to the will and ways of God. Satan never was a part of the Godhead. He was never like God, who is omnipotent—all powerful, omniscient—all knowing and omnipresent—everywhere present. Satan is not all powerful. He doesn't know everything, and he is not present everywhere at once.

However, God created humankind with the potential to participate in all the attributes of God, especially when man is moving by God's Spirit and functioning in the Spirit dimension of God's nature and attributes. Man was created with greater power, wisdom, and authority than the devil. But man fell by obeying the devilish serpent and not God, and thereby relinquished the position and power God had given humankind. The devil then made himself the god of the earth and all its evil ways. When the Scripture refers to the devil as *"the god of this world"* (2 Cor. 4:4 KJV), it is not giving him the status of being a god like the Eternal God of the universe. There is only one God. The devil is just a prince of darkness. Satan is the ruler and god of all who do not accept Jehovah's way of life and His only provision for humankind's reconciliation to God, Jesus Christ His Son.

JESUS CHRIST CREATED A NEW RACE OF PEOPLE

When Jesus died on the cross, arose from the dead, and birthed His Church, He began a new race of humankind. This race consisted of people who were born again and transferred from the curse of the earth to the blessings of the Kingdom of God. Man was reinstated and activated into a new-man-creation greater than Adam's original creation. Adam was created without the knowledge of sin and rebellion and lived a life of innocence until he partook of the forbidden fruit. The new-creation-man in

Christ Jesus was created from humankind that was not innocent but knowledgeable of good and evil. The new-man-in-Christ race, which is the Church race, was created in the righteousness of God.

The new Church race consists of saints who have been born of the Spirit and baptized in the Spirit. For as many as are led by the Spirit of God, they are the sons of God (see Rom. 8:14). Jesus is the King of His Kingdom of saints. He has given them His power and authority over all the power of the devil (see Luke 10:19). The spiritual saints are God's delegated ambassadors and warriors to implement and execute all that Christ wants His Church to be and do. The saints also have the authority to execute all the judgments that the Eternal God has decreed upon the world. The works that Jesus did while on earth are to also be done by the saints—and even greater works (see John 14:12; Ps. 149:6-9; Jer. 51:20; 2 Cor. 5:20).

EXAMPLE OF THE HELPER AIDING THE WARRIOR SAINTS

For the last twenty-four years during the month of October, we have conducted our Christian International Apostles and Prophets Conference. At this conference during Desert Shield, the buildup to the first Gulf War, God prophetically revealed that He wanted us to do spiritual warfare for the allied soldiers. The Lord revealed that the devil was planning for 60,000 American soldiers to be killed. He wanted us to intercede and war against the enemy's plans and save 50,000 of our soldiers from being killed. There were over 1,000 in attendance at the Conference.

We did spiritual warfare by first revealing to everyone participating what had been revealed to us and then directing our praying against the enemy. We spoke in the authority of the name of Jesus, made apostolic decrees and prophetic proclamations with the Word of God and the shout of faith. After we prayed with all the understanding we had on the battle, I exhorted all the saints to

WESTJET
24SEP14 FLT/VOL 3288

CROMACK/GARY MR

DEP: EDMONTON INTL AB   9:10PM

ARR: CALGARY INTL AB   10:00PM

BOARDING TIME/
HEURE D EMBARQUEMENT

8:30PM

OPERATED BY WESTJET ENCORE 0400
ELECTRONIC/ELECTRONIQUE
8382101688359/3

BOARDING PASS/ CARTE D EMBARQUEMENT
CROMACK/GARY MR
24SEP14
FLT/VOL 3288

GATE /PRT 49I

SEQ 075
PNR TVXWFZ

DEP: YEG
ARR: YYC

SEQ 075
PNR TVXWFZ

SEAT/PLACE 12C

SEAT/PLACE 12C

pray in their spirit languages in their warfare tongues. I explained how the Holy Spirit sent us a Helper, not a dictator, and that the Holy Spirit would help direct all of our different spirit prayer languages to pray for the same thing even though we would each be speaking in different spirit languages. A thousand saints speaking in tongues at the same time against the same enemy would produce more spiritual power than the Hoover Dam could produce in electrical power during the same time. The Bible says one can put a thousand to flight, but two can put 10,000 to flight. How many of our enemies could 1,000 united saints praying in the spirit put to flight? Millions of demonic principalities and evil angels were put to flight.

We did about thirty minutes of intense spiritual warfare. The shout of faith in our spirit languages exploded in the enemy's camp like an atomic bomb destroying thousands of demonic forces and disrupting their communication channels. The Holy Spirit then revealed that we had won the battle.

At the time, I wondered why God told us that He was giving us the responsibility of saving 50,000 instead of all 60,000. Two weeks later, I was preaching in a prophetic church in Tulsa, Oklahoma. I shared with them about our recent spiritual warfare that the Lord showed us was to save 50,000 of the 60,000 soldiers. They got excited and explained to me that during that same night God had spoken to their church gathering to intercede and battle for the lives of 10,000 American soldiers! That was the reason: this church was commissioned to save the remaining 10,000.

We later heard reports that tactics and plans for where to invade the land were changed at the last moment—at the time of our spiritual warfare. These changes outwitted the enemy and their demonic spirit helpers. The U.S. had shipped tens of thousands of body bags overseas, which did not need to be used. The saints had the privilege and delegated authority to win the war in the heavenlies before and during the time it was being fought with natural weapons on earth. This example should not be construed to say that everything the U.S. military does is ordained by God or that all of her enemies are demonic. But we do know that our spiritual enemy, the devil, wanted to kill tens of thousands of young men and women because he loves death and destruction, and God allowed us to war in the spirit to stop his evil plans.

Israel was God's chosen people who fought natural human enemy soldiers with natural weapons. The Church of Jesus Christ are God's spiritual warriors who fight evil spirit armies in the heavenlies. Though the Church saints are natural people with flesh and bone bodies, they are a spirit people who do spiritual warfare in the spirit world. The saints fight from their spiritual headquarters— their heavenly places in Christ, at the right hand of God. Their ability to pray in a spirit language is one of their great spiritual weapons of warfare. The spirit language is our helper and warrior maker. The saints who exercise their spirit prayer languages are encouraged, enabled, enlightened, and empowered to be mighty warriors in the army of the Lord.

OTHER EXAMPLES OF HELP IN WARFARE

These are the same principles we followed when directed by the Holy Spirit to go to the Pacific Rim nations and disrupt and stop the devil's plans to start a third world war between the West and the East. We did spiritual warfare in those nations from 1992 until 2001 when God assured us that we had accomplished our assignment. The devil's plan to start a third world war by causing the eastern nations to fight against the western nations was stopped. The devil then switched to terrorism in a major way on September 11, 2001.

We have used these same weapons of warfare when our local church has discovered that the devil has assigned an evil principality against us. We do the same when we discover the devil's plans against our Christian International Apostolic Network.

ALLOW THE HELPER TO ASSIST

This whole chapter was written for the purpose of helping Christians understand that the Holy Spirit is a Helper and not a dictator. The gift of our spirit language is the Spirit's main means of helping Christians. The Holy Spirit and our spirit language assist and cooperate with us in our work for God. If we all want to pray in unity and agreement about something, or make war against some evil force, the Holy Spirit will cooperate by directing all the spirit languages of the saints to pray for the same thing at the same time though in different spirit languages.

These are just a few of the numerous examples that could be used to show the many various ways that our spirit language can be used to help us to overcome our enemies and accomplish great things for God. Do not allow any uninformed and inexperienced Christian to talk you out of using your spirit language to its maximum purpose, power, benefits, and blessings. The Holy Spirit knew all that the spirit language was designed to do and that is the reason He chose the spirit language as the greatest gift He could possibly give to a child of God. Therefore, every Christian should receive the gift of the Holy Spirit, pray much and often in tongues, and appropriate all the benefits of "the gift" of his or her spirit language.

70 REASONS CONTINUED...

FORTY-SEVEN

The gift of the Holy Spirit is not a dictator or controller, but a "*helper.*" Other translations interpret the Greek word *parakletos* as Counselor, Comforter, and Advocate. The word Helper conveys more how the Holy Spirit works with us to fulfill our ministry and do the works of Christ. The Holy Spirit sent His gift to encourage, guide, and help us, to enlighten and enable, reveal, and instill what we need to do the will of God. He didn't come to do the work for us, but to empower us to do the works of Christ. The spirit language is not temperamental or independent of us, nor dominating over us, but one with us to help us in every way possible to fulfill our membership ministry as an eternal member of the forever-functioning Body of Christ (see Acts 1:8; John 14:26; 15:26; 16:7-15; Eph. 3:20-21).

FORTY-EIGHT

The gift of the Holy Spirit is more desirous and willing to manifest God's power in and through us than we are to receive and manifest God's grace and gifts. Incredible as it may sound, the gift is ready and willing twenty-four hours a day to assist us and cooperate with us to accomplish God's purposes. But our spirit language can only do His work as we give Him opportunity and time to pray in tongues long enough to procure what we need.

FORTY-NINE

Our spirit language from the Holy Spirit has the same warrior spirit as Jesus, the Mighty Warrior, and Almighty God who fought for Israel. The spirit language is a warrior maker. Praying in the spirit language is a vital part of the Christian warrior's armor. The weapons of our warfare are spiritual weapons and our spirit language is what empowers us to use them powerfully and effectively in overcoming our enemies (see Eph. 6:10-18; 2 Cor. 10:3-4; Josh. 10:14).

FIFTY

Praying in our spirit language activates us into our spiritual position in the heavenly places in Christ at the right hand of God. This is the saints' spiritual sphere of operation, warrior headquarters, and command center. Our position is *"far above all principality and power and might and dominion and everything that has a name in the natural world and spirit world."* The resurrected body of Jesus Christ is seated at the right hand of God, but His Spirit is with us here on earth. Our mortal bodies are here on earth, but our spirits are seated with Christ Jesus at the right hand of God. It is a mystery and paradox that we can be functioning in our natural bodies on earth while at the same time our spirits are seated and functioning from the right hand of God in the heavenly places in Christ. Praying in tongues originates and functions from our spiritual position in the heavenlies (see Eph. 1:21; 2:6; Eph. 1:3; 2:22; Col. 1:27).

FIFTY-ONE

The major weapons of warfare for the Church are the blood of Jesus, the name of Jesus Christ, the Word of God, the high praises of God, the shout of faith, and the gifts of the Spirit. The spirit language is what empowers the saints with the love, Faith, and power to use these weapons effectively (see Mark 16:17; John 14:13; Ps. 149:6-9; Heb. 4:12; Eph. 6:16; Josh. 6:20; Ps.47:1; 2 Cor. 10:4; 1 John 1:9; 4:18; 5:4).

FIFTY-TWO

When the saints are gathered and feel led to do spiritual warfare against a particular enemy or for some particular purpose, the Holy Spirit will direct the spirit languages of all the saints to pray for the same thing at the same time, even though each saint is praying in a different tongue. The power of unified praying in the spirit is immeasurable—greater power than an atomic bomb. *"Five of you shall chase a hundred, and a hundred of you shall put 10,000 to flight."* Five fighting together destroys twenty enemies per soldier, but one hundred soldiers unified destroy one hundred per soldier. *"One can put a 1,000 to flight but two can put 10,000 to flight."* Just adding one more takes it to the power of ten. *"One man of you shall chase a thousand, for the LORD your God is He who fights for you.*" We have unlimited victory when God fights for us. How much power would be generated with 500 or 1,000 people praying at one time? What if one million saints around the world agreed to pray in tongues at the same time for the same thing. We could tear down the kingdoms of the devil and build God's Kingdom over all the kingdoms of this world (see Isa. 60:22; Josh. 23:9-10; Lev. 26:8; Zech. 12:8; Matt. 11:11; Dan. 7:14, 18, 22, 27; Rev. 5:10; 11:15).

ENDNOTES

1. *The WORD: The Bible from 26 Translations* (Gulfport, MS: Mathis Publisher, Inc., 1993 latest edition), 2101.

2. *The Living Webster Encyclopedic Dictionary of the English Language* (Chicago: The English-Language Institute of America, 1971).

3. Ibid., 104.

4. Bill Hamon, *Who Am I and Why Am I Here?* (Shippensburg, PA: Destiny Image, 2005).

CHAPTER 10

THE GREAT INTERCESSOR

SPIRIT LANGUAGE—THE GREATEST INSTRUMENT OF INTERCESSION

The Word of God exhorts Christians to pray always with all prayer and supplication in the Spirit. Remember that Paul used the terms, "praying with the Spirit" and "praying in the Spirit" as synonymous with praying in tongues with our spirit language. The last phrase in the verse of Ephesians 6:18 says that we are to make prayer and supplication for all saints everywhere. Most Christians only know a small number of saints really well—such as their families and closest friends—and even among those, they may not know what is happening in their lives that needs prayer or how to best pray for them. But the Godhead of Father, Son, and Holy Spirit knows every saint everywhere and what each of their needs are at any moment in time. The resurrected body of Jesus is seated at the right hand of the Father making intercession for the saints, but His Holy Spirit is within the saints making intercession for them and through them.

> *Likewise the Spirit also helps in our weaknesses. For we do not know what we should pray for as we ought, but the Spirit Himself makes intercession for us with groanings which cannot be uttered. Now He who searches the hearts*

knows what the mind of the Spirit is, because He makes intercession for the saints according to the will of God. Who is he who condemns? It is Christ who died, and furthermore is also risen, who is even at the right hand of God, who also makes intercession for us (Romans 8:26-27, 34).

OUR SPIRIT LANGUAGE PRAYS FROM THE MIND OF THE HOLY SPIRIT

When the Scripture says that the Spirit makes intercession for us with *"groanings which cannot be uttered,"* it is revealing that the Spirit makes intercession through us with our spirit language. Our natural speech cannot articulate the inner groanings of what the Spirit within wants to express. So the Spirit makes intercession with groanings that cannot be uttered in our learned language.

To "utter" means to give expression to with the voice; to give vent to with the vocal organs.[1] On the Day of Pentecost when the disciples originally received the gift of the Holy Spirit, they spoke with tongues as the Spirit *"gave them utterance"* (Acts 2:4). To give utterance is to give inspiration and words for the voice to express; it is a meaningful speech sequence grammatically independent of the context in which it appears. To give utterance in tongues is not meaningless gibberish or senseless syllables. The Holy Spirit's gift to the believer is a spirit language that can give utterance to all those inner groanings within the spirit of a child of God. Our spirit language is the greatest source we have for intercession in the spirit or fulfilling the scriptural admonition to pray always in the spirit for all saints.

First Corinthians 2:16 declares that those who are spiritual have the mind of Christ. The Amplified Bible says we have the mind of Christ and do hold the thoughts, feelings, and purposes of His heart. The feelings and purposes of God are in our spirit, and our spirit language prays directly from those impressions, motivations, and purposes of God. The mind of Christ originates and flows from the inner mind of our spirit and not from our natural understanding. Then the truth and understanding can come into our natural mind from the Spirit of God within us. The Living Bible declares, *"Only those who have the Holy Spirit within them can understand what the Holy Spirit means"* (1 Cor. 2:14).

Using computer language, we would say that the mind of Christ is in our hard drive, which is the Holy Spirit who is one with our spirit. Speaking in tongues is the keyboard that brings the information to the screen of our minds so that the thoughts of Christ can be seen and understood. The fingers of God's Spirit are directing the keys of the keyboard. Praying in our spirit language brings the mind of Christ from the depth of the Spirit within and illuminates our understanding enabling us to think and act according to God's will and purposes. This is one of the great works of our spirit language, especially when we need wisdom and revelation on something in order to do the will of God. Romans 8:27 reveals that the Holy Spirit with the spirit language searches the heart of man to know his desires and needs, and then knowing the mind of Christ on these matters, He makes intercession for the saints according to the will of God.

OBEYING AND PRAYING WITHOUT KNOWING WHY

There are some times when the Spirit does not illuminate our natural understanding when seeking to accomplish a specific purpose. In fact, this is true most of the time when we do spirit language intercession. When we are prompted by the Spirit to intercede, we may not know for whom we are praying, why we feel such an urgency to pray in tongues, or for what purpose. The following story illustrates this truth.

I have read many stories of people's experiences that reveal this truth, but this particular story I personally heard from visiting missionaries who spoke at my Bible college. The Northrups were missionaries in a nation with areas that were uncivilized, and no outsiders—especially white missionaries—had ever been to some of the tribal areas. The Northrups felt the leading of the Lord to go way up river to evangelize a tribe that had never heard the gospel of Jesus Christ. The team of husband and wife and a few others began the long journey up the river into the depth of the vast jungle.

Mrs. Northrup had brought a big bunch of bananas and was getting ready to give one to each of the party. Suddenly natives with spears came screaming and leaping from the banks of the river and from the overhanging limbs of the trees. They took all of the missionary team at spear point to their village. The natives did not immediately kill them because they were not allowed to do anything with what they captured until the chief of the tribe authorized it.

It was quite a distance to the village, but when they arrived the team was made to stand facing the king of the tribe surrounded by warriors who were pointing spears and knives at them. The chief allowed the witch doctor to examine them to determine if they would be good or bad for the village. The witch doctor was dancing about in front of them and chanting and screaming with his mouth wide open. It was a very tense, life-threatening situation. Mrs. Northrup was praying desperately for God to save them. She asked God to show them what to do.

The Lord whispered to her to take the longest and biggest banana off of the bunch that she still had in her hand. The Holy Spirit then told her to take that banana and shove it down the witch doctor's throat the next time he came by screaming in her face. She thought, "Are you sure, God? We are in enough trouble now, if I do that they will kill us for sure!" But the Spirit prompted her more strongly. So the next time he came by and opened his mouth wide to chant his spells, she plunged that banana as hard and as far as she could down the throat of that witch doctor! He immediately fell to the ground gasping for air but could not breathe because of the banana in his throat.

Every warrior and all the tribesmen froze in their tracks in shock and astonishment at what they were beholding. The warriors greatly feared the witch doctor and were afraid to do anything to offend him. After a few minutes of silence and no one moving—except the witch doctor writhing on the ground—they suddenly heard the big king begin to laugh out loud. He then spoke to Mrs. Northrup, saying effectively, "Come and tell me about your God who makes you brave enough to ram a banana down my witch doctor's throat. When even my mightiest warrior would not dare do such a thing, a mere woman has gagged my witch doctor."

The missionary team was then able to preach the gospel to the tribe. The king was born again, along with all his people, and that tribe became a great influence for Christianity throughout that region. The missionary team was able to get back home safely and continue their ministry.

When they arrived back in the United States they shared their experience at their home church. One of the sisters came up to them and began to talk excitedly. She told them about her experience of the Lord telling her to pray in tongues until He told her she could stop. She knew by the feelings in her spirit that she was interceding for some saints somewhere for some reason. She thought about the Northrups while she was praying, but did not know for sure she was praying for them. She prayed unceasingly for four hours before she felt a release to cease praying in her spirit language. When they checked the date and difference in time zones, they discovered the sister started her intense intercession at the same time the natives captured the missionary team, and she had not ceased praying until the king and his people had accepted the Lord.

An important truth is revealed in this incident. When the Spirit of intercession rises within you with an intensity for you to pray in tongues and intercede, do not stop praying until you feel the peace of victory and the release to cease interceding. There are hundreds of other stories of Christians being used of God to intercede in the spirit for things that their natural minds did not understand. Many may never know what they accomplished until they get to Heaven.

Nothing Is Accomplished Without Prayer

There is a divine principle and spiritual law of God for the human race that we need to understand. Nothing is accomplished on earth for the cause of God without someone somewhere first praying it into existence. God is continually looking for a person who will be instrumental in interceding for His saints (see Ezek. 22:30). Jesus is at the right hand of the Father interceding for intercessors to be raised up who will take the time to allow the Holy Spirit to intercede through them in the tongues of their spirit language. Nothing is accomplished in and through the Church on earth without intercession.

That is one major reason why the Holy Spirit chose the unknown tongues of the spirit language as the greatest gift that He could possibly give to God's children. The Holy Spirit can direct millions of Christians who are responsive to the Spirit to intercede for a million different needs. Or, if a need is major enough, He can have all one million Christians around the world united in praying for the same thing at the same time. The eyes of the Lord are scanning over the earth to find those with "the gift" who are willing to pray any time the Spirit directs.

When Jesus told us to pray to the Lord of the harvest that He would raise up laborers for the harvest, part of what Jesus had in mind was for laboring intercessors. Intercessors are like midwives who help babies get delivered. Intercessors praying in Spirit-directed tongues cause souls to be saved, bodies to be healed, revival in the church, release of finances for advancing the Kingdom of God, and the list could go on and on. Prophetic intercessors are those who have learned the value of praying with their spirit language. They also receive words of knowledge and wisdom and discerning of spirits to do specific praying in their native tongues and to make prophetic proclamations for the fulfilling of God's prophetic purposes. Most powerful prayer warriors pray by presenting what they know about the situation in making their requests known to God. They then turn the matter over to their spirit prayer language to pray with the fruit and gifts of the Spirit in the will of God with full authority.

When I was a speaker at the Azusa Street Centennial, researchers announced that more than 600 million Christians have received the gift of the Holy Spirit with speaking in other tongues. If just one million of those would dedicate at least 30 minutes a day to the Holy Spirit for praying in their spirit languages, we could begin to change the world. Tremendous power would be released in the Church worldwide, and the Kingdom of God would be demonstrated in every nation as a witness to the Lordship of Jesus Christ.

Who will hear the call to be a harvest reaper and an instrument through which the Holy Spirit may intercede? The harvest is truly ripe but spirit language intercessors are far too few. I am praying that each one of you who reads this book will not just fill your head with knowledge, but your heart will be set aflame with passion that stirs your faith to take action and become a prophetic intercessor. We should count it an honor and privilege that God would gift us with a spirit language that can be the voice of Christ Jesus speaking through us making intercession for His children. This is one way we fulfill the Scripture that says we are co-laborers together with Christ (see 2 Cor. 6:1; Rom. 8:17).

CHRIST MAKES INTERCESSION WITH THE SAINTS

We are seated in the heavenlies with Christ, and Christ is at the right hand of God making intercession for the saints. I used to wonder how Jesus was making intercession for millions of saints all at once. Now, I see that He doesn't do it just through his mouth alone, but through the millions of mouths who are members of His corporate Body. The major way Jesus makes intercession is by His Spirit making intercession through us with the spirit language.

Remember we are baptized into the Body of Christ, and now we are members of the one Body of Christ of which Christ is the head. We are one with Christ for he who is joined to the Lord is one spirit with Him in one Body of Christ. We are one with everything that Jesus Christ is and does. This includes being one with Christ in His ministry of intercession where we are seated with Him at the right hand of God in the heavenly places. We are joint-heirs with Christ in all that He inherited from His Father God. When Jesus arose from the dead and birthed His Church, He commissioned His Church with everything that Father God had commissioned Him to be and do, including the ministry of spirit intercession (see 1 Cor. 6:17; Eph. 2:6; Rom. 8:17; 1 John 4:17).

The Holy Spirit gave to every member of the Body of Christ who would believe and receive the gift of their own spirit language, the ability to be one with Christ in spirit intercession. Remember what we said earlier in this book, that the majority of Spirit-baptized Christians do not understand or use more than ten percent of the power and purposes God ordained for the spirit language to do in and through the saints. May all who read this book begin to increase in the knowledge and experiential ministries of their spirit languages until they are using 100 percent of the Holy Spirit's purpose in giving the greatest gift possible for the believer.

PERSONAL BENEFITS OF SPIRIT LANGUAGE INTERCESSION

DEVOTION AND WORSHIP ENHANCED

There are many personal benefits that come from interceding in one's spirit language. It is the greatest means by which we worship God in spirit and in truth. The Spirit also intercedes for our personal needs.

The Spirit helps us in our weaknesses, for we do not know what we should pray for as we ought:

> *But God who searches our hearts knows what the mind of the Spirit is, because He makes intercession for the saints according to the will of God* (Romans 8:27).

According to the revelation in this Scripture, the Holy Spirit fully knows the deepest longings and desires of our spirit. The Spirit makes intercession to God for us through the spirit language that He gave us. Our redeemed spirit is so grateful to God and loves Him completely, but our natural understanding and words are insufficient to express the deep groanings, longings, and love in the depth of our spirit. Our unlimited spirit language is able to put into word expression all that we cannot do with our natural language. Apostle Paul declared that he could sing and worship with words he understood and he could worship and sing praises to God in his spirit language with words that he did not understand. When we praise God with our natural language it fulfills our understanding and blesses our soul, but when we praise with our spirit language it fulfills and blesses us to the depth of our innermost being. We need to worship and praise God with both our understood language and our spirit language. Both ways have benefits for the believer.

On the Day of Pentecost, all 120 disciples received the gift of the Holy Spirit and spoke in unknown tongues. Many foreign

SEVENTY REASONS FOR SPEAKING IN TONGUES

Jews understood some of the languages they were speaking and they were amazed that the disciples were speaking of the wonderful works of God. It is scriptural to exhort a congregation of Christian believers to all worship God for a period of time with their spirit languages. Most Christians do not know what to say when lifting their hands and praising God for several minutes. Many just say, "Thank you, Lord," "Hallelujah," "Glory to God," etc., but after a few minutes they run out of words and phrases to fully express the love and appreciation they feel for God. However, our spirit language has an unlimited means of expression. Many times during worship, in my mind I am thinking of the good things that God has done for me and what He will do for me, while at the same time my mouth is expressing my devotion to God in other tongues with my spirit language.

In the 1950s a restoration move of God restored the ministry of singing praises to God in melodious worship. I participated in services where waves of worship continued for hours. The worshipers would give melodious praise to God with both their natural languages and their spirit languages.

I remember one particular service, which was typical of many, that lasted for four hours. There would be about 45 minutes of melodious worship, and then the worship would lower to a hum level while three or four prophecies would come forth. Then it would gradually arise again to a crescendo of worship and praise to God. This continued for hours with waves of worship and prophecies. Many stated that it sounded like a heavenly choir singing in unison and harmony to God. Much of our expression of worship was in our heavenly language of the spirit, which has the ability to express worship in heavenly tones. Jesus said that the Father sought for true worshipers who would worship Him in spirit and in truth (see John 4:23). Worshiping with our spirit language is one of the main ways of worshiping God in spirit. *We are those who worship God in the spirit, and rejoice in Christ Jesus"* (Phil. 3:3).

SPIRIT PRAYING IS ALWAYS IN THE WILL OF GOD!

The Holy Spirit directs our spirit language to pray prayers in accordance with the will of God. Probably the only time we can be assured that we are praying 100 percent in the will of God is when we are praying in our spirit language. God always answers requests that are made in alignment with the will of God.

Now this is the confidence that we have in God, that if we ask anything according to His will, He hears us. And if we know that God hears us, whatever we ask, we know that we have the petition that we have asked of him (see 1 John 5:14-15).

The Spirit makes intercession for the saints according to the will of God. For the Spirit searches the heart of man and knows the desires and needs of man and the will of God concerning those needs and desires (see Rom. 8:27).

The Spirit only directs us to pray according to the will of God. For example, we may be praying in our understanding for God to bless us with popularity and great recognition, but when we start praying in tongues, the spirit language may start praying for God to arrange situations to bring humbleness into our lives. The Spirit may know that pride is beginning to form in us because of our present success and the praise of man. The Spirit knows that pride goes before self destruction and a haughty spirit before a fall (see Prov. 16:18). Therefore, He intercedes for us to keep us from falling and causing self-destruction. The Bible says, *"The heart is deceitful above all things and who can know it? I, the LORD, search the heart, I test the mind"* (Jer. 17:9). The Spirit fully knows the secret intents of the heart of man, but He directs our spirit language to pray according to the will of God.

SPIRIT LANGUAGE—HELPER, COMFORTER, INTERCESSOR, AND FAITHFUL FRIEND

We should greatly appreciate our gift of the Spirit, for our spirit language is what helps us with all our challenging situations. Praying in tongues empowers us when we are weak, comforts us when we are saddened by life's circumstances, intercedes for us according to the will of God, and links us to Jesus, our faithful Friend on whom we can always depend. When we do not know how to pray as we ought, we can just turn the praying over to our spirit language and the praying will go directly to the heart of the matter with the wisdom and power of God to meet the need. Our trustworthy spirit language arises as a mighty warrior and does spiritual warfare against our opposition and enemies. Our spirit language fills us with the love of God, the fruit of the Spirit, and enables us to manifest the mighty gifts of the Holy Spirit.

Now we understand more fully why Jesus told His disciples that it was best for them for Him to go away so that the Holy Spirit could come. If Jesus didn't die, resurrect, and ascend back to Heaven then He could not send the Holy Spirit, which He said would be more profitable for them than Him remaining with them in His mortal body (see John 16:7). Let us be reminded again that God's greatest gift for the world was Jesus Christ His Son. The greatest gift that Jesus could give to His Church was the Holy Spirit. And the greatest gift that the Holy Spirit could give to the individual believer was his or her own spirit language. Now we understand better why the Holy Spirit chose the gift of tongues as the best gift He could give to those whom Jesus redeemed by His own life's blood. Let us give a great big thank you to the Holy Spirit for His tremendous and all-sufficient gift.

SPIRIT LANGUAGE—OUR BEST PSYCHIATRIST

During the Charismatic Movement of the 1960s and 1970s, several professional psychiatrists received the gift of the Holy Spirit. They analyzed and evaluated what speaking in tongues with one's spirit language does for the individual believer. They not only evaluated what it did for them personally, but they interviewed many who spoke in tongues. A psychiatrist knows that the primary way he (or she) can help an individual is to have the patient keep talking visit after visit until he finally uncovers hidden things in his subconscious mind that are root causes of his mental and emotional problems. When the patient comes to know the truth about what was causing his problem, he can then eradicate it out of his life. When the patients come to know the truth, the truth makes them free. Jesus said, *"You shall know the truth and the truth shall make you free"* (John 8:32, 36).

The devil uses the hidden works of darkness in a person's subconscious mind. Hidden in the subconscious mind are traumas of the past, fears, hurts, secret sins, etc. Many Christians live their lives being influenced by these hidden things, which hinder them from living a victorious Christian life. When a person repents, Jesus forgives him of all his past sins, but many of life's negative experiences can remain embedded in his subconscious. The devil uses those negative things to torment, hinder, and keep the believer from fully enjoying, living, and manifesting the nature and character of Jesus Christ.

WHAT CAN 30 MINUTES OF SPIRIT LANGUAGE PRAYING DO?

One Spirit-filled psychiatrist said that if he could get his patients to pray for at least thirty minutes every day for thirty days, then they would not need to see him anymore. Why? Because the spirit language prays from the subconscious area of man. The Holy Spirit sheds God's light on those hidden areas of the subconscious, and then the spirit language roots them up and washes them out of the soul. As Spirit-baptized Christians we have our own psychiatrist within us. His name is Dr. Spirit Language, and his office is open twenty-four hours a day. All we have to do is show up and he will begin doing his professional work within us.

AN ILLUSTRATION OF THE SPRING OF WATER

Jesus also said that the gift of the Holy Spirit is like an artisan well that flows out like a river of living water (see John 7:38-39).

When I lived on our farm in Oklahoma, my brother and I liked to go hunting with our dogs. We wouldn't take any water with us because we knew the location of a spring of water where we were going to hunt. The opening of the spring was only a foot wide, but a gallon of water flowed out every few minutes. After a few hours of hunting we looked forward to getting a cool fresh drink of water from that spring.

Sometimes the dogs would get to the springs before we did. By the time we arrived they were lapping up the water and knocking sticks, leaves, and dirt into the spring. We drove the dogs away, but the spring water was filled with dog slobber and was muddied by the dogs jumping in it with their feet. But thank God it was a spring and not a puddle of water. As we sat there the fresh spring water continued to flow out from inside the earth. After sitting and waiting for a few minutes all the debris gradually washed out and away from the spring. The muddy area cleared as the pure water continued to bubble forth. After a while we were able to dip our mouths into the water and drink until our thirst was quenched and our bellies were full.

Speaking in tongues is like the fresh water flowing up from within the earth and out through the mouth of the spring. It washes away all that the "dogs" of life have caused to clutter and muddy our lives. As we keep praying in our spirit language, the river of life keeps flowing until everything is gone that was polluting the pure water of our souls and subconscious minds. There is great psychological benefit to a Christian who prays much in their spirit language.

PRAYING IN TONGUES GIVES DIRECTION

While I was writing this book, the television news reported a story about an eleven-year-old girl with autism-related problems who went missing. Nadia had parked her bicycle on the sidewalk and decided to go on an adventure into a densely wooded swampland that extended out for miles from the subdivision where she lived. It was a heavily wooded, swampy, alligator-infested area near Orlando, Florida. Professional rescue teams searched for her for four days, but could not find her. Even if Nadia had survived the other dangers, the rescuers knew they were running out of time because she had no food or drinking water.

A man by the name of James who attended the church where Nadia and her family worshiped was praying in English for Nadia to be found. He became more burdened and started praying in tongues. He felt impressed that if he would go looking for Nadia that the Holy Spirit would lead him to where she was. God chose the right person—James was a former military man and a skilled woodsman. He dressed properly for such a task, taking water and equipment he might need to work his way through to her. He went to the area and started walking into the woods. He continued praying in tongues as he walked and followed the inner impressions to go this way and that way. He continued on until he came to a little island of higher and drier ground, and there he found Nadia.

James then called in to say he had found her. The rescue team could not see them from the helicopter until he climbed a tree and unrolled toilet paper so they could spot him. When the search team arrived, they had to cut a path through the thick brush with machetes to get to where they were and bring her out. She was found in the large conservation area around Lake Jesup, which is considered one of the most alligator-infested bodies of water in central Florida.

The newspaper reporters interviewed James and asked him how he found Nadia when the professional search teams were not able to. He just told them that he was praying in tongues by the Spirit of God and the Lord led him right to her.[2]

There have been many reports of such things happening over the years. One of the things Jesus said the Holy Spirit would do when He sent Him to the Church was to *"guide you into all truth"* (John 16:13). Normally, we only think in terms of God leading us into all truth regarding the Church. But it can also apply to situations like Nadia's. She would have died if not found within the next day or so for she had already been four days without water. But someone dared to pray, listen to the voice of God, and have enough simple faith in God to follow his inner impressions until a lost child of God was found.

MAKE A DEDICATION

By now we are closer to understanding 70 to 80 percent of the known benefits of receiving and using "the gift" of the Holy Spirit. Our spirit language blesses and ministers to our body, soul, and spirit. Speaking in tongues charges our spirit like a battery charger charges a battery. It produces power within us like a hydroelectric power plant. The spirit language gives strength to our body by flooding our soul with the joy of the Lord, which is our strength. It blesses our soul with all of its psychological benefits. The Holy Spirit's gift to us is ready to do so much more for us than we ever give him opportunity to do.

I hope that as you fully understand the many benefits received by praying in tongues, you will take every moment you can to pray in your spirit language—when you are driving alone in your car, when you are doing housework, or during any work or activity where speaking in tongues is not a hindrance to what you are doing. May you be encouraged to get alone with God, shut away from all distractions, so that you can receive a downloading from God's computer of revelation, divine directives, and strategies. As you enter the private bridal chamber of your heavenly Bridegroom you may express fully through your spirit language your great love and appreciation for your Lord and Savior, Jesus Christ.

We are living now in the last days and the Holy Spirit has been commissioned to intensify His work with the saints. There will be more and more supernatural works of the Holy Spirit in and through the saints. Jesus is looking for those who will pray much in tongues, hear the voice of God, and obey the prompting of the Spirit within. Make a dedication now to be more sensitive to the Spirit, pray in tongues more than ever before, become a spiritual Christian, an instrument of the Holy Spirit to glorify God, do the greater works of Jesus, and demonstrate the Kingdom of God. If you fail a time or two, do not quit for you will learn by exercising your spiritual senses to recognize the voice of God accurately and take the right actions. It is better to be a fool for trying to be directed by the Spirit and failing than to be a fool for fear of trying. An army is arising of spirit-warriors who will be sensitive to the Spirit, hear the voice of God, and dare to do the impossible.

70 REASONS CONTINUED...

FIFTY-THREE

Praying in our spirit languages is the main way we fulfill the scriptural admonitions to *"pray without ceasing"* and *"praying always with all prayer and supplication in the Spirit."* Christians can pray in tongues anytime and anyplace they so desire. If we are at a place where it is not convenient or wise to speak out loud in tongues, then we can still pray with our inner man in tongues without making an audible sound. When I am walking down the concourses of airports, I speak in tongues for most of the people are speaking on a cell phone and many use the kind where they do not need to hold the phone. I just talk in tongues like I am talking on a remote cell phone and no one pays any attention to me. We can pray in tongues while driving our cars, doing housework, or engaging in any activity that does not require our voices. We can pray always in the Spirit by praying in our spirit languages (see Eph. 6:18; 1 Thess. 5:17; Matt. 26:41; Luke 18:1; 21:36; 1 Cor. 14:15).

FIFTY-FOUR

Our spirit language is the great intercessor within us. Jesus is at the right hand of the Father making intercession for the saints and the Holy Spirit is within us making intercession. Jesus doesn't do the interceding just through His mouth alone, but through the millions of mouths of those who are members of His corporate Body, the Church. The major way that Jesus and the Holy Spirit are interceding is through the language of the spirit praying in tongues through the saints (see Rom. 8:26-27, 34).

FIFTY-FIVE

When the Scripture says that the Spirit makes intercession for us with groanings that cannot be uttered, it is revealing that the Spirit makes intercession through us with our spirit languages. Our natural speech cannot articulate the inner groanings of what the Spirit within wants to express. *"The Spirit makes intercession with groanings which cannot be uttered"* in our learned language. To "utter" means to give expression to with the voice; to give vent to with the vocal organs. It requires a spirit language to vocally express in intercession what the Spirit wants to accomplish (see Acts 2:4; Rom. 8:26).

FIFTY-SIX

The Amplified Bible says in First Corinthians 2:16 that *"we have the mind of Christ and do hold the thoughts, feelings and purposes of Christ's heart."* The feelings and purposes of God are in our spirits and our spirit languages pray directly from those impressions, motivations, and purposes of God. The mind of Christ originates and flows from the inner mind of our spirits and not from our natural understanding. The truth and understanding that comes into our natural minds comes from the Spirit of God within us. Using computer language we would say that the mind of Christ is in our hard drive, which is the Holy Spirit who is one with our spirits.

Speaking in tongues is the keyboard that brings the information to the screen of our minds so that the thoughts of Christ can be seen and understood. The fingers of God's Spirit are directing the keys of the keyboard. Praying in our spirit language brings the mind of Christ from the depth of the Spirit within and illuminates our understanding enabling us to think and act according to God's will and purposes. This is one of the great works of our spirit language, especially when we need wisdom and revelation on something in order to do the will of God. With the spirit language, the Holy Spirit searches the heart of man to know his desires and needs, and then knowing the mind of Christ on these matters, He makes intercession for the saints according to the will of God (see Rom. 8:27; Eph. 4:23).

The spirit language is the believer's best psychiatrist. During the Charismatic Movement some psychiatrists and psychologists received the gift of the Holy Spirit with speaking in tongues. They analyzed and evaluated what speaking in tongues with the spirit language does for the individual believer. One Spirit-filled psychiatrist said that if he could get his patients to pray for at least thirty minutes in tongues every day for thirty days, then they would not need to see him anymore. Why? Because the spirit language prays from the subconscious area of the person. The Holy Spirit sheds God's light on those hidden areas of the subconscious and then the spirit language roots them up and then washes them out of the soul. Jesus said that the gift of the Holy Spirit would be like an artisan well that flows out rivers of living water. It is like a small spring of water that gets polluted, but as the spring keeps flowing out water from within, it washes away everything unclean and is restored back to a pure stream of water. Speaking in tongues is our artisan well and living water spring (see John 7:38-39; Rom. 8:2, 13-16).

FIFTY-SEVEN

According to researchers there are more than 600 million Christians who have received the gift of the Holy Spirit with speaking in other tongues. If just one million of those would dedicate at least thirty minutes a day to the Holy Spirit for praying in their spirit languages we could begin to change the world. Tremendous power would be released in the Church worldwide, and the Kingdom of God would be demonstrated in every nation as a witness to the Lordship of Jesus Christ. Who will hear the call to be a harvest reaper and an instrument through which the Holy Spirit may intercede? The harvest is truly ripe but the spirit language intercessors are far too few (see Ezek. 22:30; 2 Chron. 16:9; Matt. 9:37-38; 24:14).

FIFTY-EIGHT

Worshiping God in our spirit languages is one of the main ways we worship God in the Spirit. Jesus said, "The Father is seeking for those who will worship Him in spirit and in truth, for God is a Spirit and those who worship Him must worship in spirit and truth." Apostle Paul declared that, "We are those who worship God in the Spirit." Worshiping God in the tongues of our spirit languages is one of the greatest devotional benefits of receiving and exercising the Holy Spirit's greatest gift to the believer. Be one of those whom the Father is seeking (see Phil. 3:3; John 4:23-24).

FIFTY-NINE

The Holy Spirit directs our spirit language to pray prayers in accordance with the will of God. Probably the only time we can be assured that we are praying 100 percent in the will of God is when we are praying in our spirit language. God always answers requests that are made in alignment with the will of God. "The

Spirit makes intercession for the saints according to the will of God" (see Rom. 8:27; 1 John 5:14-15).

SIXTY

Our spirit language is our Helper, Comforter, Warrior, Intercessor, and Faithful Friend. We should greatly appreciate our gift of the Spirit, for our spirit language helps us with all our challenging situations. Praying in tongues empowers us when we are weak, comforts us when we are saddened by life's circumstances, intercedes for us according to the will of God, and is a faithful friend on whom we can always depend. When we do not know how to pray as we ought, we can just turn the praying over to our spirit language and the praying will go directly to the heart of the matter with the wisdom and power of God to meet the need. Our trustworthy spirit language arises as a mighty warrior and does spiritual warfare against our opposition and enemies. Our spirit language fills us with the love of God and the fruit of the Spirit and enables us to manifest the mighty gifts of the Holy Spirit. Now we can more fully understand why Jesus told His disciples that it was best for them that He go back to the Father and send them the Holy Spirit, who would bring for them His greatest gift of their own spirit language (see John. 16:7; Rom. 5:5; Exod. 15:3; Acts 9:31).

SIXTY-ONE

Praying in tongues can help us find people and things. Our spirit languages will guide us by giving words of knowledge and wisdom in our minds, or strong impressions in our spirits that motivate us to go and be at the right places at the right times. There is no limit to the ways that praying in tongues can enable us to have supernatural knowledge and do supernatural things to bless ourselves and meet the needs of others. We must allow our spirit languages to play a major role in our lives. The Holy Spirit's gift of our spirit language is the greatest friend, helper, and companion we can have. The spirit language is the greatest gift a Christian could possibly receive (see John 16:13-15; Eph. 3:16, 20).

ENDNOTES

1. Pei, *The Living Webster Encyclopedic Dictionary*, 1091.

2. Strang Communications, Inc., 2010, "Man Praying in Tongues Finds Missing Girl," Orlando, Florida. http://charismamag.com/index.php/news/26711-man-praying-in-the-spirit-finds-missing-florida-girl.

CHAPTER 11

WHO CAN RECEIVE "THE GIFT?"

THREE BAPTISMS FOR ALL

In his preaching on the Day of Pentecost, Apostle Peter established who could receive the gift of the Spirit and what the requirements are to receive the gift.

> *Then Peter said to them, "Repent, and let everyone of you be baptized in the name of Jesus Christ for the remission of sins: and you shall receive the gift of the Holy Spirit. For the Promise is to you, and to your children, and to all who are afar off, as many as the Lord our God will call"* (Acts 2:38-39).

All who are called to be children of God are to receive three major baptisms:

1. Baptism of repentance where one receives Christ into his or her life. The evidence of that baptism is a born-again experience resulting in the person living the life of Christ (see John 3:3-5; Luke 3:3; Mark 1:4).

2. Baptism in water where the old man of sin is buried, and the new man arises to walk in resurrection life (see Rom. 6:3-6; 1 Pet. 5:21; Col. 2:12).

SEVENTY REASONS FOR SPEAKING IN TONGUES

3. Baptism in the Holy Spirit where a person is filled with the Holy Spirit to overflowing in other tongues. The result and evidence of a person receiving the promised gift of the Holy Spirit is speaking in the unknown tongues of their newly received spirit language (see Acts 1:5; 2:38; 2:4).

FOLLOW THE ORIGINAL PATTERN, RECEIVE THE THREE GREATEST GIFTS

The New Testament Church doctrine and practice was for everyone who received Christ to receive water baptism and the baptism of the Holy Spirit. Apostle John declared, *"There are three that bear witness on earth: the Spirit, the water and the blood, and these three agree in one"* (1 John 5:8). We receive the witness of the blood with the baptism of repentance, the witness of the water with water baptism, and the full witness of the Spirit with the baptism in the Holy Spirit. Jesus told His followers to go into all the world and make disciples of all nations baptizing them in the name of the Father, Son, and Holy Spirit—representing the three baptisms of repentance, in water, and with the Holy Spirit.

God the Father gave the gift of His Son and requires everyone to repent and accept Christ in order to become a child of God. Jesus, the Son of God, died on the cross and shed His life's blood for the remission of sins. Water baptism in the name of the One who died for all, Christ Jesus, identifies the new child of God with the death and resurrection of Jesus Christ. The Holy Spirit baptizes believers with the gifted ability to pray in a spirit language. The gift of the Holy Spirit is the divine ability given to a Christian to pray in the tongues of their spirit language anytime there is a need or they so desire. That spirit language becomes a part of the new Spirit-born person's nature, character, and capability, enabling him to pray in tongues anytime he wills to do so. A believer can pray in tongues as he wills, the same as a natural-born person can willfully speak in his learned language.

If a person receives God's greatest gift for all the benefits Christ's eternal life brings and if a person receives the Holy Spirit Jesus gave to His Church and all the benefits He brings, then they should definitely receive the gift that the Holy Spirit gives to the individual believer and appropriate all the benefits the spirit language brings.

HOW TO RECEIVE THE GIFT OF THE HOLY SPIRIT

The gift of the Holy Spirit is received the same way one receives the gift of eternal life. First, you must receive revelation and understanding that the gift is for you. It was promised to those who originally received, to their children, and to all following generations during the entire time of the Church Age.

Second, you must have the confidence that whatever you ask the Lord for is exactly what He will give you. Jesus promised His disciples, *"Whatever you ask in my name that will I do for you"* (John 14:13-14). And He promised if you ask for the gift of the Holy Spirit that is exactly what He will give. Our Heavenly Father is absolutely trustworthy (see Luke 11:13).

Third, you must receive by faith. When you asked Jesus to forgive you of your sins, you had to believe first that when you asked for forgiveness that you would receive it and have the assurance that you would be born again. You had to believe with your heart and confess with your mouth to receive salvation. (If you have not yet received salvation, you can pray right now and be born again.) When you ask for the gift of the Holy Spirit, you have to exercise the faith to begin speaking in other tongues. As you are receiving the gift you will feel certain impressions in your spirit and sense certain sounds and syllables in your mind and speech. You have to allow these things to form into a language and by faith speak forth your new gifted language of the Spirit (see Heb.11:6).

THE SPIRIT DOES THE GIVING, BUT THE BELIEVER DOES THE SPEAKING

The Holy Spirit imparts the ability into your redeemed spirit. The spirit language originates in your spirit and flows out of your innermost being. God does the giving, but you have to do the speaking. It is not an operation of the natural mind. Some people do not speak in tongues because they think the Holy Spirit does the talking. They are waiting for Him to sovereignly take control of their tongues and force them to speak. But the Bible says, *"And with many other words he testified and exhorted them, saying, "Be saved from this perverse generation"* (Acts 2:40). The Holy Spirit does not need to speak in tongues for He knows and understands every language in Heaven and earth. It is the children of God on earth who need the ability to pray from their spirits directly to God who is a Spirit. The saint of God needs the spirit language for all the benefits it brings.

Some experience great emotional joy and excitement when they receive the gift. Others do not have any emotional experience whatsoever when they receive their spirit languages. However, as they continue to pray day after day they begin to experience many positive spiritual emotions at different times. Once you receive the gift you can activate praying in your spirit language by faith, meaning it is not dependent upon soulish emotions or physical sensations. Remember, the gift of the Holy Spirit is not the fruit of the Spirit of joy, peace, etc., nor is it the gifts of the Spirit; it is your spirit language, which has the ability to produce the fruit and gifts of the Spirit.

WHY ALL CHRISTIANS DO NOT RECEIVE THE GIFT

The main reason not all Christians receive the gift of a spirit language is the lack of knowledge that the gift is for every Christian and not knowing the many valuable benefits of a spirit language. The reason most Christians do not know these things is because their pastors do not preach it. *"How then shall they call on Him in whom they have not believed? And how shall they believe in Him of Whom they have not heard? And how shall they hear without a preacher?"* (Rom. 10:14). The reason many ministers do not preach about receiving the gift of one's spirit language and its benefits is based on their understanding and relationship in the origination, deterioration, and restoration of the Church.

STANDARD DOCTRINE AND PRACTICE

Preaching about the gift of the Holy Spirit was standard practice of Apostle Peter and Apostle Paul in the book of Acts. The book of Acts demonstrates the doctrines and spiritual manifestations of the New Testament Church ministers and saints. Teaching on the gift of the Holy Spirit and praying for saints to receive and practice praying in the tongues of their spirit language was standard among Early Church ministers. A proof example is Apostle Paul's teaching in First Corinthians 12–14. This section includes one chapter on love and two chapters devoted to teaching on speaking in tongues and the gifts of the Holy Spirit. That is much more than Paul devoted to teaching on communion of the bread and wine; guidelines for being single, married or divorced; fivefold ministers, what to do in a complete church service; worship and singing in church; and many other ordinances still practiced in twenty-first century churches. The baptism of the Holy Spirit with speaking in tongues was also included in the six foundational doctrines of the

Church. The third doctrine of the six is the "doctrine of baptisms" which includes the three basic baptisms of repentance, water, and the baptism of the Holy Spirit (see Heb. 6:1-2).

PERSONAL HISTORY AND TESTIMONY OF RECEIVING THE GIFT

If we could read the personal testimonies of the approximately 600 million Christians who have received the gift of the Holy Spirit, we would find that all 600 million are in some way unique. The bodies of all human beings have the same members located in the same areas of the body—two eyes and one nose in the front of the face and so on. Yet, no two human beings are exactly alike, for even the fingerprints of each person are different. In like manner, everyone receives the gift of the Holy Spirit the same way, *"by grace through faith,"* yet each one has his or her own unique testimony.

My journey of being a born-again, Spirit-baptized Christian began in the middle of the twentieth century. On the night of July 29, 1950, I received my born-again experience. That was the day of my sixteenth birthday. I had been riding my horse two miles to attend a brush arbor meeting every night for three weeks. It was being conducted in the country five miles out from the small town of Boswell, Oklahoma. I had no exposure to Christianity prior to this time. The singers and preacher at the meeting read out of a book they called a Bible. I checked with my Mom to see if we had such a book. We found an old Gideon's Bible with the back torn off, but all the pages were there. I began reading to see if what they were saying was in the Bible. I discovered it did talk about a Heaven and a hell and people getting saved and talking in tongues. At that time I had no idea what that all meant, but it was in the Book.

A Birthday Gift Used to Activate a Spiritual Gift

When the meeting was finished that night, my girlfriend gave me a wrapped birthday gift, which I tied on the back of my saddle. I then walked her home a mile in the opposite direction from where I lived. After riding three miles back home, I unsaddled my horse and fed him some corn. I then knelt down in the corn crib and lifted my hands and prayed as I had been doing for the last two weeks. This night of my birthday would prove to be different. When I got in the house and opened my gift, there was a beautiful new Bible in the box. Somehow God used that Bible as a catalyst to open my heart for Him to come in. Suddenly the Holy Spirit came into my life, and this time as I prayed something happened. I was born again by the Spirit of God.

Receiving the Gift

The next night, at the end of the preaching, they gave the same persistent altar call for people to come forward and receive Christ Jesus. I went forward with my girlfriend and three other teenagers. As I knelt and began praying, I saw a vision of Jesus hanging on the cross speaking to me that He died for me so I might live with Him. As I was viewing this scene, words were pouring out of my mouth. In my natural conscious mind I was expressing thanks to God and telling Jesus that I would live for Him. The preacher began to pray for me and then he started saying, "That's it, just speak it out." I wondered in my mind what he was talking about for I was talking as loud and fast as I could! When he talked about me speaking, I suddenly realized I was not talking in English but in a language I did not understand. I realized it must be those "other tongues" that the Bible said the disciples prayed in on the Day of Pentecost. Such joy and excitement flooded my soul with this speaking in tongues that I continued speaking in my new spirit language for almost an hour. The following Sunday we all met at the river and the preacher baptized me in water.

That all happened sixty-two years ago, and I have continued to pray in tongues. I will pray more and more in my spirit language as long as I am in this mortal body. Since I discovered all of the valuable benefits of praying in tongues, I can say with Apostle Paul, *"I thank God I speak in tongues."* I have experienced all of the seventy reasons given in this book for speaking in tongues. I now understand what Paul and Peter meant when they wrote, *"We thank God for His unspeakable gift,"* and *"We rejoice with joy inexpressible and full of glory."* It is a gift that cannot be spoken in our learned language, and the joy of the Lord that cannot be fully expressed with our natural language, but it can be fully expressed with our spirit language (see 2 Cor. 9:15 KJV; 1 Pet. 1:8; John 15:11; Matt. 25:23; Neh. 8:10).

FAMILY RECEIVING THE GIFT

My wife's parents and grandparents were tongue-talking Christians. Evelyn was saved at age three and received the gift of the Holy Spirit when she was seven. She was filled with the Spirit for quite a while before she had faith to speak in tongues. One night a woman of God was praying with her at the altar to receive the gift. Evelyn was hesitant about speaking what she was sensing and hearing in her spirit. She was afraid that it would just be her repeating what she had heard others speaking or sounds she was just imagining. The sister who spoke with her at the altar gave her scriptural assurance that Jesus would give her a language of the Spirit that was from God. So Evelyn began to speak what she was sensing in her spirit and mind. Within a few minutes she was flowing like a river in her spirit language. That was sixty-eight years ago and she is still praying in tongues to this day.

Our three children, who are now ordained ministers, got saved before they were five years old and received the gift of the Holy

Spirit by the time they were seven. All of our eleven grandchildren were saved and received the gift of the Holy Spirit with speaking in tongues between the ages of three and nine years old. All of our nine great-grandchildren who are over three years old are saved and filled with the Holy Spirit. From Evelyn's grandparents to our great-grandchildren makes six generations, covering more than eighty years, of tongue-talking Christian families.

POSITION IN RESTORATION DETERMINES ONE'S REVELATION!

In my 380-page book called *The Eternal Church*,[1] 173 pages give detailed information concerning the restoration movements that have taken place during the last five centuries. From the Protestant Movement, which officially began in A.D. 1517, to the Saints Movement, which I believe history will show began in 2007, there have been 490 years of Church restoration movements. A "reformation" includes many restoration-of-truth movements. My most recent book prior to this one brings the revelation that the *Third and Final Church Reformation* began in 2008.[2]

The First Reformation birthed the Church, established it, and took it into all nations. There were eight major moves of the Holy Spirit to accomplish God's purpose for the First Reformation. The Church then had a great falling away and descended into a Dark Age for approximately 1,000 years, from A.D. 500 to A.D. 1500. Almost all of the teachings and spiritual experiences of the early apostolic Church were lost or converted to religious ritual during this time.

The Second Reformation, which many historians call the Protestant Reformation, began the period of the great restoration of the Church (see Acts 3:21). God's purpose for this reformation was to restore all New Testament teachings, spiritual experiences, and supernatural ministries that had been present in the Early Church back into the Church. There have been eight major restoration movements in the Second Reformation to accomplish God's progressive and ultimate purpose for His Church. The Second Reformation progressed the Church in restoration until the Church was ready to be launched into the Third and Final Church Reformation. The Third Reformation will fulfill God's ultimate purpose for His Church.

WHY DENOMINATIONS EXIST

All mainline Christian denominations are in existence because of one of the restoration movements. For example, the first restoration movement was called the Protestant Movement. Martin Luther wrote ninety-five arguments against the unscriptural religious practices of his Christian denomination (Catholicism) that had developed during the Dark Age of the Church. Luther received the revelation that we are not saved by religious works but by the grace of God and the accomplished work of Jesus by His death and resurrection. The result of the Protestant Movement was the establishment of many Christian denominations: Lutheran, Presbyterian, Anglican (known as Episcopalian in the U.S.), and a few other, lesser-known groups.

The Evangelical Movement, which began about 1600, taught on water baptism by immersion. This produced all the different Baptist denominations and some Puritan groups, Quakers, and others. The Holiness Movement, which was started in the 1700s by John Wesley, taught on holiness and victorious Christian living. It resulted in many holiness groups such as the Methodist, Nazarene, and Church of God denominations. The Divine Healing Movement of 1880 restored the truth of divine faith healing for the physical body of humankind and resulted in the formation of the Christian and Missionary Alliance denomination to carry on that truth.

None of the previously mentioned movements had received the revelation and assignment to restore the truth and spiritual experience of the gift of the Holy Spirit with speaking in other tongues. God's time for that was the next progressive restoration movement in 1900, which became known as the Pentecostal Movement. Numerous Pentecostal denominations were established from the restoration of this truth. The better-known ones are the Assemblies of God, Foursquare, Pentecostal Church of God, Church of God in Christ, and United Pentecostal Church. Millions of Christians have received their spirit languages in these Pentecostal churches over the last one hundred years.

The Charismatic Movement (1948-1988) is an inclusive term covering the Latter Rain Movement, the Charismatic Renewal, and the Faith Movement. All of the truths and spiritual experiences of the past movements were reemphasized at this time, plus many new truths and spiritual ministries were added. During the Charismatic Renewal, the truth of baptism in the Holy Spirit with the ability to speak in a spirit language was taught by some in the older denomination churches. The Prophetic-Apostolic Movement, which started in the 1980s, restored the function of the prophet and apostle back into the church, as well as ten other major biblical teachings and spiritual experiences. The Saints Movement, birthed in 2007, is teaching the activation of every saint into being a minister in his or her sphere of influence. The gifts of the Holy Spirit are being activated in the saints so they can demonstrate the Kingdom of God in every nation. (This is fully explained in my 400-page book *The Day of the Saints.*[3])

The Third Reformation is designed to activate all restoration truth, spiritual experiences, and miraculous manifestations into the Church. This is for the purpose of demonstrating the Kingdom of God as a witness of the sovereign Lordship of Christ Jesus. The Third Reformation has recently begun and will continue until Jesus returns and the kingdoms of this world have become the kingdoms of our Lord Jesus and His Church (see Rev. 11:15; Matt. 24:14).

UPDATE AND ACTIVATE

The purpose of this minute presentation of Church restoration is to show why all those in Christendom do not teach and practice speaking in tongues. If you became a Christian in one of the restoration churches that was first established before the Pentecostal Movement, then you were probably not taught that the gift of the Holy Spirit with speaking in tongues is for you to receive. This is because this revelation was not part of their restoration truth, and therefore never became a part of the established doctrine and practice of that denomination. All Pentecostal denominations and independent Pentecostal networks and ministerial organizations preach and practice speaking in tongues. Regardless of what denominational or church background you come from, all Christians need to update with the Holy Spirit's restoration of truth and let Him activate all restored truth and ministries into their lives.

EVERYONE CAN RECEIVE

Every child of God needs to receive the Holy Spirit's greatest gift of a personal spirit language and derive all the numerous benefits and blessings of praying in tongues. The other great benefit is the power it gives to live the life of Christ and minister the supernatural gifts to the Church and to win the lost to Christ Jesus. The gift has been restored. It is available to whosoever will obey God's command to believe and receive their spirit language. It is God's revealed will for everyone to receive the gift of the Holy Spirit. Who can receive the Holy Spirit's gift of the spirit language? Everyone who has received Christ Jesus as their personal Savior. Just hear the truth about the gift of the Holy Spirit, believe and receive the gift by faith, and then speak in tongues by the empowerment of the Holy Spirit.

70 REASONS CONTINUED...

SIXTY-TWO

Everyone who receives Christ Jesus as their personal Savior is qualified to receive the gift of the Holy Spirit. It is promised to all who live during the Church Age, which started with the first coming of Christ and continues until His second coming. If a person receives God's greatest gift for the benefits that His gift of eternal life brings, and if a person receives the Holy Spirit Jesus gave to His Church and all the benefits He brings, then he should definitely receive the gift that the Holy Spirit gives to the individual believer and appropriate all the benefits the spirit language brings (see John 3:16; Acts 2:38).

SIXTY-THREE

The Holy Spirit's gift is the divine ability given to a Christian to pray in unknown tongues with a new spirit language. The gift includes the ability to pray in tongues anytime there is a need or desire to do so. That spirit language is a gift given to a Spirit-born person. To be "given" means that it becomes a part of a person's inner spirit being's nature, character, and capability, the same as a natural born person's learned language becomes a part of his speaking ability (see 1 Cor. 12:7; 14:15).

SIXTY-FOUR

How does one receive the gift of the Holy Spirit? The same way the gift of eternal life was received: believe in your heart and confess with your mouth. Believing in your heart makes you right with God, but speaking with your mouth possesses the gift. After reading this book you should be convinced that the Holy Spirit's gift of the spirit language is for you. Follow the four principles for activation listed in Chapter 7. As you are receiving the gift you will feel certain impressions in your spirit and sense certain sounds and syllables in your mind and voice. Allow those divine impressions to form into the language of your spirit and you will begin speaking in tongues. You have now received, continue to pray in tongues every day and derive all the valuable benefits the Holy Spirit put within the operation of the gift. Remember you have received the greatest gift the Holy Spirit could give from all of God's resources (see Rom. 10:8-10).

SIXTY-FIVE

The reason all Christians do not understand, receive, Preach, and practice the gift of the Holy Spirit is based on when their denominations were formed during the last 500 years of the restoration of God's truths and spiritual experiences to the Church. The revelation and restoration of receiving the spirit language of the Holy Spirit did not take place until 1900. The Christian denominations that were formed during the first 400 years (1500-1900) of restoration of the Church did not include the validity of receiving the gift of the Holy Spirit with speaking in tongues within their denominational doctrines and practices (see Acts 3:21; see also *The Eternal Church*[4]).

SIXTY-SIX

Every child of God needs to receive the Holy Spirit's gift of his or her own spirit language. It is a commandment of Jesus Christ for Christians to receive the gift. It is the greatest gift given for empowering the saints of God to live the life of Christ and manifest the greater works of Jesus. The gift has been restored. It is for all believers regardless of what denomination they belong to. During the Charismatic Renewal, Charismatic groups were formed in every Christian denomination. Today God is giving a new urgency and emphasis on the gift of the Holy Spirit. It is not an extra gift, but a necessity for Christians to fulfill God's purpose for His last-generation Church during the Third and Final Church Reformation (see Acts 1:4, 8; John 14:12; Zech. 4:6).

ENDNOTES

1. Bill Hamon, *The Eternal Church* (Shippensburg, PA: Destiny Image, 1981, 2003), 151-193.

2. Bill Hamon, *Prophetic Scriptures Yet to Be Fulfilled* (Shippensburg, PA: Destiny Image, 2010).

3. Bill Hamon, *The Day of the Saints* (Shippensburg, PA: Destiny Image, 2002).

4. *The Eternal Church*, 151-193.

OTHER INTERESTING REASONS

70 REASONS CONTINUED...

SIXTY-SEVEN

Scientific studies have been done on people speaking in tongues. Dr. Andrew Newberg compared brain scans of Christians praying in tongues, Buddhist monks chanting during Meditation, and Catholic nuns praying. The study showed quite different results between those praying in tongues and the others. The frontal lobes—the part of the brain right behind the forehead that is considered the brain's control center—went quiet in the brains of the Christians talking in tongues. As the nuns prayed and the monks chanted, that part of their brains became more active. The discovery that Christians' frontal lobes go neutral while they are speaking in tongues proves that speaking in tongues is not a function of the natural brain, but an operation of the spirit. "If I pray in a 'tongue' my spirit is praying, but my mind is inactive" (1 Cor. 14:2, 14 PNT).

SIXTY-EIGHT

Praying in tongues enters us into the rest prophesied in Isaiah 28:12. The spirit language releases what is needed to give us the peace of God which surpasses all understanding. We cease from our laborious praying in our learned language(s) and enter into the rest of allowing our spirit language to do the praying, which activates the fruit of the Spirit and the grace of God into our soul, which consists of our mind, will, and emotions. Numerous people have testimonies of being specially sustained during great tragedies and traumas by praying in tongues. The spirit language actually activates the blood and glands of the body to produce what the body needs. Praying in tongues relaxes us into His rest. The children of Israel did not enter that rest because they "did not obey." The Holy Spirit's gift is given to those who obey. The spirit language is that place of rest (see Isa. 28:11-12; 1 Cor. 14:21; Heb. 3:18; 4:8-11; Acts 5:32).

SIXTY-NINE

Ezekiel prophesied that the Church is to get in water deep enough to swim in. If you have a room you want filled with water and you have many water faucets in the room that are connected to an endless reservoir of water, then all you have to do to fill the room with water is to turn the faucets on and let them flow until the room is filled. Our tongue is like the water spout. The Holy Spirit within us is the endless reservoir. Talking in tongues turns the water faucet on, so that rivers of living water flow out of our innermost being. We can all pray in tongues until the room is filled with the water of God's presence and glory (see Ezek. 37:5; John 7:38).

SEVENTY

There is nothing more valuable than being in unity with God and His people. We are to keep the "unity of the Spirit." Unity is not everyone being in one organization or one family or one gathering of church people. Unity is a spirit function that requires God's Spirit to produce true unity. Psalm 133:1 says, *"How blessed it is for brethren to dwell together in unity, for there God commands His blessings and life forevermore."* When the disciples became unified in one mind and purpose, then suddenly the Holy Spirit came and baptized every one of them. The spirit languages that the Holy Spirit gave the disciples activated them into a unified divine flow of their spirits with all that speaking in tongues produces including the unity of the Spirit.

CONCLUSION

Praying in tongues produces harmony and unity within us, with God, and with our fellow saints. Jesus prayed that we might be one in unity as He and the Father are one, so that the world would believe. If everyone would pray in tongues and let it activate the unity of the Spirit, then it would help fulfill the prayer of Jesus for the members of the Body of Christ to become one. How blessed we are to have the unity producer within us. What an awesome responsibility we have to allow the spirit language to accomplish all God's purposes, appropriate all His benefits, and empower the saints to live the life of Christ and demonstrate the power of God and Lordship of Jesus Christ. Amen and Amen. (See Ps. 133:1-3; Eph. 4:3; Acts 2:1; John 17:20-23.)

ABOUT DR. BILL HAMON

Dr. Bill Hamon is co-founder with his wife, Evelyn, of Christian International Ministries (CI) which is involved in apostolic oversight in churches around the globe and has a world-wide presence in education and training. His many years of ministry experience provide a balanced, biblical approach to church restoration with focus on the offices of the prophet and apostle.

Dr. Hamon's family stands as a testimony to his character. He has been married fifty-seven years. Their three children and their spouses are ordained ministers, working full-time with them in the ministry and giving them eleven grandchildren and nine great-grandchildren (two more on the way) who are joyfully serving the Lord. This speaks loudly of the man, his message, and his ministry.

In addition to national conferences and ministry engagements wherein he personally ministers to thousands each year, Dr. Hamon has written several books revealing and bringing church restoration to the forefront, including *The Eternal Church, Prophets, Pitfalls and Principles, The Day of the Saints, Prophetic Scriptures Yet To Be Fulfilled,* and *"Apostle Prophets and the Coming Moves of God".*

Dr. Bill Hamon, Th.B., Th.M., D.D., is respected by church leaders around the world as a senior leader of the prophetic/apostolic company God is raising up in these last days.

» 62 years as a born-again, Spirit-filled, baptized Christian.

» 60 years as an ordained minister and has prayed for tens of thousands to receive the gift of the Holy Spirit.

» A Bishop to over 3,000 ministers and churches around the world.

» Bishop and his ministers have taught and trained over 250,000 Christians in spiritual ministry.

Through his fifty-eight years of ministry, Dr. Hamon has gained much insight to the value and purpose of praying in a spirit language which has enabled him to develop these seventy reasons for speaking in tongues.

1,000,000 SPIRIT LANGUAGE WARRIORS

Read again Chapter 10 The Pages under Heading "Nothing is Accomplished Without Prayer" and Reason #57!

BE ONE OF THE 1,000,000

We are believing for One Million Saints around the world to pray thirty to sixty minutes every day in their spirit language; What power could we produce?

The Challenge goes out to:

» Individual Christians

» Apostles of Networks

» Pastors of Churches

» Watchman Intercessor Lists

» Non-Profit Organizations

» Facebook Friends

Everyone who has a list:

Contact them to commit to praying daily thirty to sixty minutes in tongues. Keep reporting to drbill@bishophamon.org the count of people that have committed to being an instrument of the Holy Spirit for thirty minutes every day.

The Holy Spirit wants 1,000,000 saints to pray thirty minutes a day in tongues with the spirit language that He gives to each believer.

IN THE RIGHT HANDS, THIS BOOK WILL CHANGE LIVES!

Most of the people who need this message will not be looking for this book. To change their lives, you need to put a copy of this book in their hands.

> *But others (seeds) fell into good ground, and brought forth fruit, some a hundred-fold, some sixty-fold, some thirty-fold* (Matthew 13:8).

Our ministry is constantly seeking methods to find the good ground, the people who need this anointed message to change their lives. Will you help us reach these people?

> *Remember this—a farmer who plants only a few seeds will get a small crop. But the one who plants generously will get a generous crop* (2 Corinthians 9:6).

EXTEND THIS MINISTRY BY SOWING
3 BOOKS, 5 BOOKS, 10 BOOKS, OR MORE TODAY,
AND BECOME A LIFE CHANGER!

Thank you,

Don Nori Sr., Founder
Destiny Image
Since 1982